J. Gordon Kingsley

"Blessed Harlaxton, My Home"

Beloit, Wisconsin
Turtle Creek Publications
2015

Turtle Creek Publications
2067 W. Collingswood Drive
Beloit, WI 53511
gordon.kingsley3@gmail.com

ISBN-13: 978-0692398005 Turtle Creek Publications)
ISBN-10: 0692398007

In Honor of

SUZANNE

Despite all,
Through all,
Because of all,
She Made It Happen.

And Harlaxton is a better place.

Contents: "The Bits and Bobs"

Preface and Acknowledgments

These sketches come from the pleasant solitude of our most agreeable house-in-the-woods on Turtle Creek, in Beloit, Wisconsin, USA.

They were written during the first few months after retiring from work as Principal of Harlaxton College at the end of June, 2014, after nearly twelve years of serving the lively, lovely community that is Harlaxton. "Senior Citizens" have told me that "getting old is not for sissies." Well, neither is retiring, when you love your work and the place where you work. But, as one of these sketches suggests, there is also something deeply good about finishing up, and summing up, and celebrating good work done well. These essays are part of that celebration.

They are also a loving farewell to Harlaxton and her people.

The title comes from a work written for the Harlaxton Collegiate Choir by our then-choirmaster, Professor Sally Brown, in 2007—she called it simply "The Harlaxton Song." Suzanne H. Kingsley, whose volunteer work for Harlaxton is celebrated in the Dedication and in one of these sketches, was kind enough to read the manuscript, though she is no way responsible for any of the content. And by far my most encompassing acknowledgment is owed and offered to those successive communities of good people who have been my forebears and colleagues at Harlaxton College herself—staff, students, faculty, donors, friends—who have built themselves a fine little American College on ageless English ground. (You know who you are, and I hope you know how much I admire you, appreciate you, even love you.) These intrepid seekers and learners and doers and givers have marched across Harlaxton history, making the place "go," but more important, making the place "sing."

I penned these words. But they wrote the song.

Gordon Kingsley
New Year's Day, 2015

Harlaxton: All Together

"Okay, okay, what are you all about, really? I mean, a patchy batch of American students coming to a glorious British manor house for 'college in a castle'? Get serious.

"It's really an excuse to travel, isn't it, on someone else's money? Get serious.

"What are you all about, really?"

He asked me with a straight face, this cynic of an American professor "just passing through" on a summer junket of his own (on someone else's money!)   And I, as Principal of Harlaxton College, answered him straight-faced and head-on, in words something like this:

"What we are about is education, and education of the highest order — intense and personal and total. We've got it all together, or are getting there. 'X-treme! Education,' it is.

"For Harlaxton is a different, and a special, kind of place.

"No drive through, cheap mind-meal Mcstudy. No College Lite. No fragmenting, no splitting apart, of the living and the learning — or for that matter, of the working and the traveling and the playing. At Harlaxton College, the learning involves everything we do. At Harlaxton College, the learning never ends. It is continuous, each part of Harlaxton life reinforcing and complementing the others in a grand, interactive drama of grasping new truth and new life.

"So, the great Harlaxton Manor House is itself a teacher, as we live in it, all 153 rooms — it is our home! As are the tough courses, as are the exciting travels, as are the experiences of living and dining together, as are student-created activities, as are sports (everybody can play on the Harlaxton Lions teams!), as are connections with local host families and churches and schools and community.

"Because all of us live in our great Harlaxton Manor, because we are a small and close-knit group, because   all of us take the same core course in British Studies and read the same set of books (all the student body and **all** the British faculty and many of the American faculty — everyone — in the same beautiful room--the Harlaxton Long Gallery--for the same lecture at 8:30 every Monday and Wednesday), because all of us are exploring in a "new" old world, because faculty and students are in close daily contact all the time — not just in class sessions — for hey! we eat together, drink together, play together, talk together — we are the whole thing, the real thing. The opportunities for an intensified learning are remarkable, indeed.

"At Harlaxton, we are a true collegium — a gathering of those more knowledgeable and experienced with those less so, living and learning together around the great ideas of a great culture.

"It is heady stuff, and we take it on it with right good zest — together."

It is Harlaxton. It is College.

The Harlaxton Experience.

This was printed in **The Crescent,** a University of Evansville student publication, March 4, 2004.

Getting There—and Back: Talking about the Weather

It's a miracle, really.

Every semester—that's every single semester—we managed to get a couple of hundred students and visiting faculty from America to Harlaxton. And every time, every time, we got them home again. I was always amazed when it happened.

Just think about it: each and every semester, students were to come from thirty or more airports in the United States, sometimes from other countries on other continents, and they were to make the necessary changes in flights at God-only-knows what airport or airports in God-only-knows what city or cities, then to get on some transatlantic flight with God-only-knows what airline, and land at Heathrow Airport in London by 10:30am on the prescribed day for us to pick them up in big buses ("coaches") and take them to Harlaxton Manor. And this drama was played out in the lives of 150 to 175 students, and 30 or more faculty family members, every single arrivals day of every single semester. A computer whiz could probably calculate the possibilities for disaster and the sum would be enormous.

Add to this the fact that only a few persons each term were experienced travelers. Most were not. Some had never even been on an airplane.

But it worked! They showed up!

Oh, there were glitches—winter storms, summer storms, a volcano blowing its top in Iceland, mechanical trouble on any single aircraft at any single airport, which could delay connections with domino effect through a whole itinerary. And not knowing things, even though our written and spoken instructions clearly spelled them out—like the fact that Terminal 5 at Heathrow was miles away, indeed a train ride away, from the Terminal 3 pickup point. And unforeseen problems like people running their cell ("mo-bile") phone batteries out of power with chit-chat, then not being able to call the couriers who were meeting the flights, or Mum at home, or the Harlaxton reception desk, or anywhere else when the phone was really needed.

But in it all, Harlaxton students showed a remarkable resilience, a remarkable ingenuity, remarkable bursts of courage and independent, imaginative thinking. The result was that every student arrived at Harlaxton, and back home again after semester, every...single...time.

We even lost our capacity to be surprised by episodes of bad weather somewhere in America, for compared with smaller Britain, weather in the USA is much more violent much more often in many more ways in any season. And we learned that the airlines, and our students, would ultimately overcome all.

Over the years, I began to believe that simply Getting to Harlaxton was the First Big Lesson, the First Big Achievement, in studying abroad.

Once at Harlaxton, the weather became a non-factor. Only one winter of our near-twelve years at Harlaxton did snow stay for a while—and it was gentle, not nasty. Most years there might be a dust of snow, the grass still green under the white stuff, and then it was gone. It might feel cold because of the wet climate, but I remember Wisconsin-Eau Claire students arriving in a time of British snow, being told by the Brits how bad the weather was, and giving it a shrug and that "You ain't seen nothin'" look. If you have just arrived from Eau Claire, Wisconsin, in January, it feels balmy at Harlaxton!

We actually liked the British climate and miss it now that we are back in America (in Wisconsin, no less), though the Brits thought it was we who were balmy and not the British weather. It is, comparatively, so mild in the UK, so temperate, so gentle, so civilized, so Brit. Even the rain is usually "soft," though plenteous, and thunderstorms are rare. I may have seen lightning once in near-twelve years, maybe twice.

Time to go home at semester's end? Well, let's just run the video backward. Going *into* the storms, *into* the potential delays, *into* the flight connections, *into* the vast land of America with the weather glitches to be found only in a country so massive that it takes up all the east-west latitude of an entire continent.

But in the dozen years, we had only one real system-problem with students' home going, and that one was because of European and not American weather issues. I remember it well.

My wife Suzanne and I were leading 30-40 of our Harlaxton students on the Rome-Florence-Venice trip at end of semester and found ourselves dancing through Venice in the middle of one of the most beautiful snowfalls our eyes had ever seen (soft white snowflakes *themselves* dancing on the canals and palazzos and churches of Venice, settling as a luxurious Venetian winter cape on one of the world's most graceful cities). The problem was, this beautiful snow was falling on the day we were bringing our students back from Venice to London, where on the next morning they were to catch their flights to America.

"*Nessun problema,*" say the Italians. "No problem. Planes are still flying." And so we take our happy, weary, now-eager-to-get-home group to Venice's Marco Polo Airport for their British Airways Flight 2587 to London Gatwick Airport. Marco Polo is a nice airport, and it's good that it is—for we wait, and wait, and wait, watching the snow pile up on runways and aprons. Finally, finally, our British Airways aircraft arrives from London, then manages to take off again and return with us all aboard—the last flight able to leave Venice during this most unusual storm. We land in Britain about midnight, only three hours late. And I promptly check on morning flights to America.

"No problem," say the Brits. "Flights will leave as scheduled." And so Suzanne and I get our students by coach from London Gatwick to London Heathrow Airport and then we ourselves return to Harlaxton as planned, offering fond farewells to some of our students who are going to hotels for the night and to other brave ones who have made a kind of corral, a little compound with their bags, planning to sleep at Heathrow before flying out next morning.

Wrong! It is only that next morning, a hundred miles away at Harlaxton, that we hear the news flash, *"No flights are leaving Heathrow."* It turns out that the airport's much-vaunted, much advertised new runway-clearing equipment—advertised, in fact, in that very week's Heathrow newsletter as protecting that great world airport from shutdown—can in fact clear the runways very nicely, but cannot get the parked airplanes free from their gates and out *to* the runways. (Hey, guys. Talk to the people at Chicago O'Hare!)

We immediately offer free rooms and meals for any of our kids who wish to return to Harlaxton until Heathrow is operating again. But Harlaxton kids are not dummies: they know planes are not flying out of Harlaxton, but out of Heathrow; Christmas is approaching; parents are worried and vocal; and so our students stay in London.

And now a character study emerges from this weather problem. As far as I could tell, there were three distinct groups of students, three distinct sets of responses and results.

Group 1 were positive, clever American kids who, as soon as flights were moving again, read the Departures boards and showed up at every gate of every flight going to America, flashing that American charm and aw shucks helplessness, nicely chatting up the harried airport staff saying how much they hope to get home for Christmas to be with Mom and Dad and Little Sister, smile, smile, smile—and within two days everyone in this group was home. If there was an empty seat, a no-show on any airplane (and there were many), one of our kids got the place.

Group II went to airport hotels, whined a lot to Mom on the phone, cried a lot on each others' shoulders, bemoaned the injustice of a God who would put them in this fix, waited for the airline to call, and were in airport hotels for another week. A mother of a girl in that group wrote to me saying, "I despair of ever seeing my daughter alive again." But she did.

Group III. Well, these guys just went into London and partied for another week. They too got home, when all flights were flying again. Just a bit the worse for wear. Merry Christmas.

When all was said and done, I think every person got home by Christmas day, except for maybe one intrepid traveler from Alaska, who arrived home on what the Brits call "Boxing Day" — the day after Christmas.

So in the end of all, again, it was a miracle. Everyone arrived where he or she was supposed to be, wanted to be.

Conclusion? Mostly, our hoped-for miracles arrive on time, despite the weather.

This one was just a bit delayed.

"Mr. Kirk"

Students call him "Mr. Kirk."

His friends call him "Earl." Those of us who know his secret identity as a sort of superman say, reverently, "Big Earl." And we know at least some of the phone booths where he changes roles.

For all of the time that we served Harlaxton, January 2003 through June 2014, Earl was the Director of Study Abroad/Harlaxton, based at the University of Evansville. (All the time, that is, except for just a few months when the legendary and lovely Suzy Lantz was transitioning into retirement.)

That sounds nice, doesn't it. Nice title — "Director of Study Abroad/Harlaxton." Nice job. Probably interesting work. Nine to five, maybe. Maybe get to travel overseas now and then. Nice work if you can get it.

Except that, for Earl it was not just a *job*: it was a *calling*. A calling of the highest order.

I suspect he has gone at 'most everything in his life that way — growing up on a farm and in the village of Sugar Grove, west of Chicago (Isn't that lovely? There should be more "Sugar Groves" in the world!); going to the excellent Illinois Wesleyan University; studying French in graduate school at Indiana University; teaching at Southwestern College in Kansas and then Baker University, near Kansas City and nearer Lawrence. "Mr. Kirk" settled in to teach French at Baker, but they wouldn't leave him alone: he was tapped at one time to be Registrar, at another time to be Acting Dean of Academics, and at all times was a leader in a very good faculty.

Then, he was asked by Stuart Dorsey to come to the University of Evansville and manage overseas study, including recruiting students for Harlaxton College from Evansville and our twenty-five Partner Colleges and Universities (about 55-65% of Harlaxton students come from the University of Evansville; the remainder come from these superb Partner schools, most notable numbers from Western Kentucky University, Baker University, the University of Wisconsin-Eau Claire, Eastern Illinois University, Texas Lutheran College, and Texas Woman's University). Stuart had been Academic Vice President at Baker, then served Evansville in the same role, now is President at Texas Lutheran.

It was Stuart who hired me as Harlaxton Principal. And it was Stuart who hired Earl to "hold the ropes" at home for our work in England. Thank you, Stuart.

And now I get to the point of it all.

I mentioned that Earl did not accept this role as a job, but as a *calling*. A *calling* often forces a person to be *driven*. And Big Earl, as much as any person I have known, has driven himself to make a difference in the lives of students and faculty members—through their life and work at Harlaxton College.

Earl knows that lives are changed at Harlaxton. And he has got the people to the changing room. Semester after semester, year after year, working against or around all manner of limitations and obstacles, he has not only endured but also prevailed. He has delivered record high numbers to the Harlaxton program, keeping the place going and also—well, I don't know any other way to say it—changing lives for the good.

I've watched him work with students and faculty. He is charming. He is articulate. He is totally knowledgeable. He is organized. He knows what is important. He talks education, not just "good times," with the kids as well as the faculty, for he is first and last an educator. (And Harlaxton needs a genuine *educator* in this role, not just a salesperson. Believe it. I know.)

Suzanne and I have also gone on vacation ("hols") with him. In France. Nice to go to France with Earl, who speaks French like a native and even gets up early to fetch the baguettes and pastries before coffee is made. But the revelation to me has been that *the man never stops*. To tell you the truth (and momentarily to drop my happy pose of false humility), it is hard to outwork me, hard to outwork Suzanne, but I've seen Earl do it regularly! And all the while on "hols." Why? *Because the work needed to be done, and there was no one else to do it, and it mattered so much.*

Earl doesn't suffer fools gladly, and there are a lot of us around. Good for you, Earl. Instead of wasting time on some of us nimnods, Earl just worked. Earl never had sufficient staff for the important work he did, the strategic role he filled, and so he just worked nights and weekends as well as days. Earl never had sufficient budget, and so he used his own resources, found ways to make do, squeezed more blood out of every conceivable turnip, including himself—and he got the job done. Not just passably, but spectacularly. Consider this:

> The University of Evansville is 7th in the entire nation in students studying abroad—that was largely Earl's work.

> Harlaxton has consistently had full or near-full enrollments of very good students—that was Earl's work.

> And in a perfect example of poetic justice, such as seldom seen among us mere mortals, Harlaxton was named by Best College Reviews as **Number One among "The 50 Best Study Abroad Programs"** from American colleges and universities—this happening in January 2015, the month of Earl's retirement. That's #1 in America. And that, too, was Earl's work.

My daddy always said, "If you have a big job that needs doing, send a man big enough to do it."

That would have been Big Earl.

That would have been "Mr. Kirk."

The Bubble

"Welcome to Harlaxton." "Welcome to your new home." "Glad you are here." "Welcome to Harlaxton." "Welcome home."

Over and over we would murmur the words, Suzanne and I, standing at the Great Oak Front Door of Harlaxton Manor, shaking each student's hand, making clear eye contact, greeting each and every one individually, personally, as he or she stepped from the buses that had brought them from London Heathrow Airport to this their first entrance into their new home, Harlaxton College.

They were entering The Bubble.

That's not what they felt at the moment. What they felt right then was a great weariness from a day and night on airplanes, and a great sense of awe. They were entering "Grantham Castle," as one owner called it, a majestic stately home, some of them smiling and whispering "Hogwarts." And they were not just visitors: this was *their* home, *their* school, *their* front door! Pinch self. Is this real?

Yes. Indeed. It was for them, and Harlaxton is for every student and faculty member, really, really, really, really real.

For one thing, it is in **Real England**. The farms, the rolling hills, the woodlands, the small towns and villages like Grantham and Harlaxton and Denton and Croxton Kerrial and Woolsthorpe are true England, the England of calendars and post cards and dreams—not only American dreams, but the dreams of every Englishman. Yet, it is only an hour away from that "other country" called London, one of the truly great cities of the world.

For another thing, it is **Real College**. I'm sorry to say it, but some overseas study programs are College Lite, substituting travel for serious academic work in the classroom, substituting a kind of slapdash buddy system for serious teaching or serious student support. I must confess that I myself perpetrated such atrocities a time or two, years ago, as a young professor, in a January-term that we called "Winterim," our drama class traveling to London,

Paris, and Dublin (a pity it wasn't in the spring, when we could have called it, more accurately, "Mayim," rhymes with *Mayhem*).

Now even these lesser experiences can have value, but they don't hold a candle to a Harlaxton, a **real** college with **real** classes and **real** academic demand, so that as Principal I would repeat again and again and again, every day at Harlaxton, to students and to faculty, "Academics Are Job One." Yes, we traveled, and the Harlaxton trips were great trips; and so we simply co-opted the travel for our teaching and learning. We knew our priorities: "Academics Are Job One."

Not only is Harlaxton a Real College in its serious academic emphasis, but it is "real" in the sense of being a "full service college." Some overseas programs are "set-down" efforts—a prof takes students from Brand X University to London, say, they "set down" off the bus, they stay in a hostel, they have a class or two in a rented room with said prof with maybe a part-timer brought in, eat at McDonald's, line up for tickets to *Guys and Dolls*, and—voilà—they feel they have been immersed in British life and culture, when in fact in their heads and appetites they never left America. Contrast that with *real* residence life in a *real* (and magnificent) college home—an historic English manor house, with a *real* food service and a *real* clinic with doc and nurse and counselor available and a *real* religious life program and a *real* sports program and a *real* student development (student life, student affairs) program and a *real* travel program that is truly world class. Not only that, the *real* professors are available 24/ 7—for they live in the same majestic house as the students. *Real* appointments can be made with these *real* professors in their *real* offices, or the student just might talk with them over lunch ("I know we're not supposed to do business at meals, but I have just a quick question . . . .")

'Welcome to Harlaxton. Welcome to your new home. Glad you are here. Welcome to Harlaxton. Welcome home.

"You are entering a world where your classroom offers exciting and engaging learning. You are entering a world where your travel offers another kind of exciting and powerful learning. And you are entering a world where we link the two together, one experience reinforcing the other, so that the effects are powerful and transformational, which is teacher-talk for life-changing."

All of this happens in what students begin to call, after four or five weeks, "The Bubble" that is Harlaxton Manor and Harlaxton College.

Now, "The Bubble" can also have a negative meaning, and does with some who don't understand it or who misuse it. For the Manor holds 150-175 *American* students, with not many students from other countries except as they are enrolled in American universities. Although all on the Harlaxton staff are British (in the modern multicultural sense of "British"), and though British professors teach at least half the academic work of every student, nevertheless it is an American social environment, with the College organized on an American system so that students don't lose credits or time toward graduation. An American "Bubble."

The orthodoxy in study abroad programs from American schools calls for "cultural immersion" — enrolling directly, for example, in an English or French or Italian or Latvian or Brazilian or Moroccan university. This can be a very good thing if the student is ready for it. It can be a bad thing if trouble comes and there are insufficient support systems for that student.

In my years at Harlaxton, we always felt we had the best of both worlds: a demanding, supportive environment where serious academics were linked with educational travel to achieve an unusually powerful educational effect, yet the freedom and the encouragement and the support to engage local cultures in Britain and farther afield. That it was working could be seen in any weekend check out sheet: at random, I am reading the list from one long weekend in November when fifty-five Harlaxton students went with us to Paris on the College-sponsored trip, while independently, on their own, other Harlaxton students went to the four corners of Great Britain, Europe, and beyond: Barcelona, Athens, London, Amsterdam, Prague, Oxford, Berlin, Inverness, Lille, Zermatt, Leeds, Ireland, Edinburgh, Copenhagen, Rome,

Interlaken, Iceland, Lyon, Tuscany, York, Stratford, Stockholm, Cambridge. All this on one weekend!

The Bubble did indeed enclose and protect, but The Bubble also opened out transparently to the great wide world. That's why we would sometimes say, with all sincerity and based on much experience, that Harlaxton College was *the best study abroad program in the world.* Other knowledgeable people agree: *Best College Reviews,* for example, in its January 2015 ranking of "The 50 Best Study Abroad Programs," placed Harlaxton at #1. That's #1, First Place, Numero Uno. Can't do better than that! See it for yourself at **http://www.bestcollegereviews.org/best-study-abroad-programs/?**

What was the result of this great security matched with great opportunity, as The Bubble offered? Time after time we heard it, time after time we saw it, time after time we experienced it ourselves, until it became a refrain in our souls:

"Harlaxton changed my life!"

"Welcome to Harlaxton. Welcome to your new home. Glad you are here.

"And Welcome to the Whole Wide World.

"Because Now It Is *Your* World."

The Cult

"British Studies. Aagh!"

I can guess, based on some considerable experience, that this would not be an unusual response as students prepare to pack up and come to Harlaxton College.

For they didn't come to Harlaxton in order to take British Studies, much as our self-absorbed academic values might have wished for them to do so. They rather came to live in that great manor house and to travel — at least that's what they told us when we asked them in anonymous surveys, and consistently so. Honest little critters!

But, coming, they knew that we required them to take "British Studies" — six credit hours of it, which was for most of them half their academic course load at Harlaxton. They accepted this "burden" — with all the optimism of youth — as a price they had to pay to be where they wanted to be, to do what they wanted to do.

And they discovered, semester after semester, year after year, what a great course it is. I speak from experience of several years as a Lecturer in the course, and for all 11½ years of my time at Harlaxton as a "student" in the course. Even as Principal I attended lectures every semester, "missing class" only when I had to become or to impersonate the College Leader. "Took the course" twenty-three times. Guess I never passed it, though almost everyone else did, and with good grades.

And that's part of the story.

But to back up a bit: "British Studies" is the central, core course in the Harlaxton curriculum — officially, "The British Experience from the Celts to the Present Day." It is interdisciplinary, team-taught by four British professors, their doctorates (as I write this in December 2014) from some of the very best British universities: East Anglia, London, Nottingham, and Oxford. The course is required of every student and attended by many Visiting American faculty and spouses, so that much of the College is present in the Long Gallery every Monday and Wednesday morning at 8:30 for the formal lecture sessions.

Because the course carries six hours of credit, it is "life or death" to the Grade Point Average that means so much — almost everything — to the American student's academic record and future opportunities. Since the course is unfamiliar to most students not only in content but also in style, it is scary. Since Brits are doing the teaching *and the grading,* gosh oh golly gee whiz who knows what can happen — these people are *foreigners* (until we arrive, when we become the *foreigners*). Since every student takes the course, it defines the rhythms and pace, the liturgies and litanies (I choose these words carefully), of academic life at Harlaxton — which means *all* of life at Harlaxton. We even "jerked the calendar around" to make the course field trips work, even "stole" some of the precious travel Fridays from students in order to further their British Studies learning via field trips to Lincoln and London. It is a serious academic enterprise, this British Studies course, and we were serious about it.

All this could have spelled disaster for Harlaxton enrollments, for the course defies all the patterns and expectations of contemporary students in a contemporary university.

For one thing, at first look the course is simply not relevant to today's students. (Or, as one of my Freshman English students used to write it, "revelant." She was the one who would write of "this modern world of today in which we live now." "Currently." "At this point in time." Redundancy being a virtue to the young.)

So, a required course neither *relevant* nor *revelant.* Aagh!

It doesn't tell you how to get a job.

It isn't part of any academic major.

It is not about America (oh, yes, there is a mention of that slight unpleasantness in 1776, and an owning up to the fact that the United States did participate a bit in two world wars, but the USA is seen as a nation among many, and this is *British* studies).

It is not "gee whiz get with it" in style, doesn't try to help students find their "really really really true selves." It does not shape the subject matter to what the students want to hear.

In fact, the course depends heavily on the traditional professorial lecture, the professor offering what he or she is convinced the students *need* to hear. "Aagh!" you say? And the lectures can be cumbersome — not dull, usually, but cumbersome — held as they are in the long, narrow (though splendid!) confines of the Long Gallery, where those in the back of the hall can scarcely see the faces of the lecturer or the images on a large screen. The lectures and lecturers are generally excellent, and we tried very hard to make these events a direct communication between teacher and learner — eschewing [for example] those "outlines" on the screen that both professional and pitiful speakers like to throw up [sic], choosing rather to show large images that illustrated the words of the lecturer; and also installing stanchions of lights that would illuminate the face of the lecturer, so that nuances of the professor's expressions could be seen.

And massive amounts of reading were assigned. In books! The course is *not* media intensive, though it takes advantage of media both in the formal lectures and in the seminar group discussions that follow. At each session, students are held accountable to have read the assignments. In books! Aagh!

The course is not happy-clappy flexible. None of this "it's the first day of spring can we meet outside or have the day off." Like the Roman legions which marched across Britain, so this course marches relentlessly on, hour by hour, day by day, week by week, ordering all, conquering all, replacing a muddled and wild society with an ordered and orderly civilization inside the student cranium.

And the course is demanding. "But I'm not feeling well today." "I understand, but here in Britain we 'just get on with it.' We do the work we have to do, and that includes our British Studies preparation." Aagh!

As a brilliant Harlaxton Visiting Professor recently wrote me (Dr. Chris Hanlon of Eastern Illinois University and now of The New

College of Interdisciplinary Arts and Sciences at Arizona State University), "That course defies every precept currently in ascendency in U.S. higher education. In many ways, it's a travesty. Everyone should take it."

By the end of semester, most students agreed: "Everyone should take it." You would think they might have hated it, even rebelled and said, "Hell, no, we won't go." In an age of consumerism in the academy as well as in government and business and everywhere else, a rebellion could have had some considerable effect.

But, instead, a most gratifying thing happened: students were first curious, then interested, then intrigued, then seriously engaged, then in the end of all successful, then triumphant. They had conquered the damn thing. That monumental challenge called "British Studies" lay happily mastered at their feet, and they were the aspiring St. Georges who had slain that dragon. They had taken on one of the biggest academic challenges in their young lives and had *won*, learning more than they ever thought they could have learned, knowing more about British history and culture than the locals knew (said the locals). And in the course of learning about Britain, they were developing skills and insights and methods and habits of mind that will serve them well for the rest of their lives. Their honor, their native intelligence, and their almighty Grade Point Averages were intact and affirmed!

How could this be?

Well, British Studies is—simply stated—a brilliant course. It is well thought out, carrying the brands and imprints of several generations of very talented British faculty members, many of whom began at Harlaxton and went on to distinguished academic careers in British and American universities.

Its professors spare no effort in keeping it and themselves "fresh" in the offering. That is true of every single British faculty member I worked with over those near-twelve years—an astonishing thing to be able to say about any group of professionals anywhere. Every . . . single . . . one. Some of us may have been a bit quirky in our personal behaviors during those years, but *never* did that include sloughing off the work at hand. Nor, in fifty years in higher education, have I ever known a small group of four professors to produce the amount of scholarship these folks turned out year by year, led currently by their Team Leader Dr. David Green, who had already published three books before Yale University Press released his very original *The Hundred Years War: A People's History* in November 2014. The totally committed British profs goad and guide and challenge each other, support each other, work on the course together, work on their teaching effectiveness together, and the results speak for themselves.

These professors also work with and care for their students-- personally. You hear a lot of pious talk in a lot of colleges about "close personal attention to students," when in fact many professors don't want to be bothered. But in British Studies at Harlaxton College, students are at the center ("centre") of it all. I watched in amazement when the professors voluntarily began inviting their students to turn in drafts of papers in advance of due dates, using those drafts not for judgment but to *teach*, reading and commenting on every one, then reading them again when formally submitted, this time grading ("marking") them. Did you get that? These profs voluntarily doubled their work in order to teach their students when they were most teachable. And this carried through consistently — the teachers were available, helpful, demanding much, expecting much, but also giving much of themselves. I was always astounded at the standing ovations accorded these professors on the last day of lectures (see below) and at our Valedictory Dinner. Students knew and appreciated.

The course has a disarmingly simple attraction: "We study where we are." Not just that we keep up our studies, but, powerfully, we are living in and visiting the very places we are reading about in our books. So, off our students would go to London for some of the world's best theatre and music, to a Florence Nightingale Museum, a Freud Museum, the Houses of Parliament, the Globe Theatre on a very site where Will Shakespeare himself acted and produced his plays, to the exact spots where scientific discoveries were achieved, authors wrote, history was made. It is not only Dr. Samuel Johnson who knew that "he who is tired of London is tired of life."

Or with Professor Graham Baker to Woolsthorpe Manor, ten miles from Harlaxton Manor, home of local farm boy Isaac Newton, age twenty-three, who in a plague year away from his studies at Cambridge "discovered" or worked out the Laws of Motion, the Theory of Universal Gravitation (the apple trees are still there), the Calculus, and some major theories in Optics. Not bad for sixteen months of "independent study." "I was," he later said with typical British understatement, "in the prime of my age for invention." (Though he was never a very good farmer.)

Or maybe my favorite example: on the first weekend at Harlaxton most students and faculty went to London on a College-sponsored trip. And this could happen:

> First, they could **SEE** Magna Carta, two of the four original copies left in the whole world—for free, at the British Library. This on a Friday or Saturday, their choice.

> Second, after a visit to Hampton Court Palace (where Henry VIII and Elizabeth I and James I and William and Mary lived, where Shakespeare performed in his own plays, where the King James Bible was commissioned) we would stop at the meadow of Runnymede, on the Thames upriver from London, where they would **STAND** at the spot where the Barons had forced King John to sign Magna Carta. This was Sunday.

> On Monday, back at Harlaxton, their British Studies seminar was about Magna Carta, a lesson many of them had been **STUDY**ing while on the coaches to and from London, Hampton Court, Runnymede. That's unbelievable learning:

Saturday: **SEE** Magna Carta, an original copy.
Sunday: **STAND** at Runnymede, the original place.
Monday: **STUDY** Magna Carta in class.
And learning suddenly comes alive!

How could a student not be "turned on" by reading it, seeing it, touching it, absorbing it not only in the books but in "real life." It is powerful learning of the first order. Now no longer "Aagh!" But "Ah," or "Aha!"

And so, on the last day of the British Studies class, when the faculty finished that final lecture by showing a montage of images that students had seen through the semester (accompanied by stirring "Great British" music), you could literally feel the students' swelling pride as in split mini-seconds they recognized the pictures on the screen and what they meant, then recognized how much they had learned, then recognized how it had come about, then erupted spontaneously in a standing ovation for their British professors who had brought them to this point! It was a stirring moment, and I can never keep proud and joyful tears from my eyes when I think on it again.

I used to joke with our British Studies professors, though quite seriously, about their being priests and priestesses in a worthy, benevolent "cult" that nurtured this "powerful learning of the first order." They administered the "sacred" Harlaxton ceremonies of British Studies lectures and seminars, they interpreted the "sacred" texts of that "sacred" course, they led the "sacred" pilgrimages to places being studied, and they even prosecuted a good bit of "sacred" missionary work, as I am doing here, touting the merits of the course. The result: every semester, year in and year out, a cadre of very capable students was "converted" to better and deeper learning. That's what college is all about.

When all is said and done, I think that is a very good summary for British Studies: "powerful learning of the first order."

And more, it is a good summary for Harlaxton College: "powerful learning of the first order."

And even more, none of this could be accomplished without the fervor and intensity and purpose and commitment that are akin to that of a religion, a benevolent cult.

That's why, that's how Harlaxton, and these great British professors, could replace an initial "Aagh!" with an amazed "Aha!"

And, forever and ever, "Aaaah!"

Amen.

Holy Library!

The Harlaxton Library was sacred space to me.

For one thing, it was always warm—one of two places in the Manor where a person didn't have to shiver in the wet English winters when the winds were whipping south all the way from Scotland.

But that's a small thing.

The purpose of Harlaxton was/is Learning. Period. Travels to new places, growing more independent, awakening to personal gifts and maturities—all of these were very, very important. But at the end of the day, we were all about Learning.

That means books. And computers. And media materials. And people to help in using them, accessing them, opening up the mysteries, unlocking the lore.

And so we put our faculty offices, and our librarians' offices, and our Manor computer lab, and our seminar rooms right up next to our library collections—slap up against each other, not even a stone's throw away, not even a brisk walk away. A deliberate shuffle could do the job. We did this intentionally, on purpose, as serious educators teaching through our arrangement of spaces.

And we never closed the doors on all this library lore. It was there, ready, simmering, close, at hand, twenty-four hours a day, seven days a week. "Our library never closes, our minds never close," I would say all-too-frequently.

Knowing the power of the books in our own library, it was no surprise to me to ponder how early Christians collected their sacred writings, as have people from all of the world's literate religions. No surprise that the little monks labored for years in their cold scriptoriums, breathing on their hands to keep them warm so the words could be written. No surprise that the printing press changed the world, and the computer even more. As the Nobel

Prize-winning Irish poet W. B. Yeats wrote, in just the tenth line of his *Collected Poems*, "Words alone are certain good."

Yes, the Harlaxton Library was sacred space to me, despite the pizza boxes that sometimes littered it. It was where Man, or Woman, met Word. It was where learning became personal, lore became life. It was where newly-discovered knowledge hit, clicked, rang out, happened!

All hail to Priestess Jan, or Priestess Linda, or whatever College Librarian made it work for many of us. Thanks be to God for the books, and the space — and even the warmth.

Holy Library!

Her Honour, Jan

The Judge was our Librarian!

One of the great good true things, to me, of working at Harlaxton College was the privilege of working with Jan Beckett.

"Mrs. J. K. Beckett," then of the village of Ropsley, applied for the Librarian's job at Harlaxton College in a letter of "3rd August 1977," in which she wrote — with the honesty and clarity that, among other good qualities, made her the best colleague in the history of the world — "It will be noted that I have no formal qualifications in librarianship . . . ." She then proceeded to make the case why she should be hired, was hired for the princely sum of £2,100, responsible "for book purchases, budget controls, cataloguing, ordering and selling textbooks, College archives, supervising Work Study students, and other such duties as may occur during the course of the year."

Jan Beckett served Harlaxton for thirty-four years, taking on more and more responsibilities: for computer labs, audio-visuals, and all learning resources; as Director of Academic Services; as Director of Summer Programs; and finally as Vice Principal for Academic Services and Member of the Administrative Cabinet.

Along the way, she made it all work for four of the then-six Harlaxton Principals — Graddon Rowlands, Angus Hawkins, Robert Stepsis, and your obedient humble servant. The Principals would write of her valuable advice and counsel, of how she met all challenges "firmly and wisely." And Dr. Stepsis wrote of her "sagacity." I like that word, "sagacity" — it has sassiness and bite to it, as well as wisdom. It is Jan.

But here's the thing: Jan would, by agreement, leave her Harlaxton work one day a week and sit as a Magistrate — appointed by the Lord Chancellor — on the judicial bench at Magistrate's, Family, and Crown Courts, in Grantham and in Lincoln Castle. She was highly respected as a judge, as well as a Harlaxton colleague, being elected to the Bench Executive Committee.

When I was a new Harlaxton Principal and learned that Jan was a Magistrate, I sashayed down to her office next to the Library and half-whimsically asked what I should call her. With equal half-whimsy she replied, "If you were in my courtroom, it would be 'Your Worship.' But here at Harlaxton, 'Jan' is fine."

So I called her "Jan."

But my heart always murmured, and still does,

"Your Worship."

Ceremonies

You never say, "Oh, that's *just* a ceremony."

Just like in literature, or religion, you never say, "Oh, that's *just* a symbol." Or, "Oh, that's *just* a myth."

The fact is, **we define ourselves by our ceremonies**. They tell other people who we are, what we value. Possibly even more important, they tell *us* who we are, what we value. They are Identity expressed through Ritual. They are Dreams, Aspirations expressed through Tangible Actions and Words. Why else spend all that money and time on weddings, or graduations, or church services, or even things like theatre and symphony concerts or sitting in the seats in Arrowhead Stadium or Lambeau Field.

And notice that the pronoun is plural — *we*. There are individual, personal rituals and ceremonies, of course, and these are important, too. But usually, when we say "ceremony," we are talking about something we do together, as a group — a family, a college, a church, a team, a country. That's why we often feel uplifted after a convocation or church service or wedding or graduation or beating the Dallas Cowboys. *We* did certain things *together*, and the results somehow made us better *individually*, as *persons*.

It all sounds philosophical, doesn't it. Though it probably won't win me a Nobel Prize, or even a Pulitzer.

Doesn't matter. Somehow, along the way, this fact sank deep into my marrowbones and became, almost instinctively and intuitively, part of my collegiate leadership — first at William Jewell College, then at Harlaxton College.

So shortly after arriving at Harlaxton we purchased, out of our own pockets, a set of twenty-five "Harlaxton robes," academic regalia for our faculty to wear. And we made the first meeting with all our students a "Convocation Exordium" in the Long Gallery (if Harlaxton's builder Gregory Gregory could use Latin on the front of the Manor, we could use it inside). This special ceremony marking a new beginning — this "Opening Convocation" — was carefully scripted. It included the playing of British "pomp and glory" music at beginning and end, and it featured a processional and recessional by our faculty wearing those very robes. The marching in and out was led by Billy James the Master Bagpiper, by a student marking our steps with the beat of a Bodhran Drum, and by other students carrying flags of the United States of America, of the United Kingdom of Great Britain and Northern Ireland, and of Harlaxton College (we also had to buy the flags and provide the drum, the latter purchased in Donegal Town in Ireland).

British Studies professor Dr. Edward Bujak agreed to be our Master of Convocation and did a splendid job. We sang the National Anthems of our two countries — the Americans sneaking looks at their programs for the words to "God Save the Queen," the Brits doing the same for "The Star Spangled Banner." We carried forward a ritual of introducing our faculty to their students and of the Principal giving an "address," which became further ritualized (and introduced the element of some serious fun) with the singing and playing of "The Garden Song." And, it being Britain (maybe the best spot on planet Earth in the staging of ceremonies and the practice of civil or civic religion), we invited our local Church of England Rector to come, in full clerical regalia, to offer a ceremonial prayer at this beginning of our Harlaxton studies.

Sounds like a lot of hassle, doesn't it. (We even repeated it at the end of semester for a few years in a lovely "graduation" ceremony at the Harlaxton Village Church; then when there wasn't enough room in the church any longer we carried on the presentation of traditional "Writs of Achievement" around the tables of a Valedictory Dinner in the Long Gallery.)

Why, then, take the time and trouble?

Well, I said it all up top. These ceremonies said to us, ever so subtly but ever so powerfully, that we were doing important work in a magnificent historic place — the world-shaping work of teaching and learning. They said to us that we were the people who were *able* to do this work, and that we were the people *responsible* to do this work. They said to us that we were in it *together*. They said to us that we mustn't, as the Brits say, "let the side down," that we were *responsible to one another* throughout the semester. They said to us that we would *work hard*, they said to us that we would *have fun* doing it, and they said to us that the results would be both *important and good*.

Now that's a mouthful, a cranium-load, to come from a few robes and a processional/recessional and some pipes and drums and flags and some rituals of music and words.

But it worked. We knew in our hearts of hearts, in our bones, in the core of our being, who we were — we had seen it, heard it, felt it. And now we were living it.

We were now **Harlaxton!**

Changing the world, one person at a time — starting with ourselves.

Billy James and His Magical Bagpipes

You can hear him coming, and it stirs the blood.

Down the blue-carpeted steps of the great Cedar Staircase he marches, then into the Long Gallery, elegant with its gold and marble appointments and century-old wood floors and paneling. He leads a colorful academic procession: a student beating the procession on an Irish Bodhran Drum; student flag bearers carrying the colors ("colours") of the United States of America, the United Kingdom of Great Britain and Northern Ireland, and Harlaxton College; and--in dignified robes and rank--the Harlaxton College Faculty taking their ceremonial places as symbols of wisdom and truth. Or at least of knowledge.

It is Billy James, bagpiper extraordinaire, a champion competitor in the Scottish Highland Games, and Master Piper to Harlaxton College.

Few students know it, but he is also our pest control man.

Billy and his wife Anita are remarkable human beings. Just good folks from the nearby village of Ropsley. Making a living as a bug man. Making a home. And making magic with his bagpipes.

For When It Is Time, Billy James dresses in the splendor of his Scottish regalia, warms up his pipes, and makes the magic happen. He plays us into the highlands of our hopes and dreams and resolves. We *will* be our very best. We *will* make our semester at Harlaxton a turning point in our lives. We *will* make this world a better place.

Billy's music stirs our souls. His pipes stir our spirits. We are ready: Bring us New Worlds, Old Worlds to conquer! We. . .will. . . prevail! That feeling is no doubt why the English decreed in 1746 that bagpipes were an instrument of battle and that playing the bagpipes was an offense punishable by death. "The bagpipe is the only musical instrument deemed a weapon of war because it inspired its troops to battle and instilled terror into the enemy.

The skirl of the pipes stirs men's and women's souls and its power and influence in battle as in life, is measurable." [Piperalpha, "Bagpipes Are a Weapon of War," **Canada at War Forums**, January 2009.]

That's what the academic writer *says*. But Billy James *does* it. Does it all. He clears out the bugs from Harlaxton Manor. (I almost said "pests," but there were too many of us to make that possible.) And then he dons his regalia, tunes up his pipes, and leads us into the future of our dreams and goals.

Billy and Anita have two daughters, Sarah and Penny, both of university age, both studying for Music Performance degrees in Greenwich, London, in cello and violin. Why am I not surprised that one has already been featured in the London *Evening Standard* and has recorded for the BBC, is now writing and recording her first folk album, while her younger sister has already been star soloist in Vivaldi's *Four Seasons* with the Lincolnshire Youth String Chamber Orchestra.

These girls grew up knowing how to blend the hard work of everyday life with the skills, and the sounds, that dreams are made of. And they are already excelling, making their own dreams come true, while inspiring the dreams of others through music that changes lives and changes the world.

It's all there in the James family home, as it was for me in our great blessed Harlaxton Manor home, where Billy James with his bagpipes always led us to the good, to the better, to the best.

Skirl On, Billy James.

And Thank You.

"The Garden Song"

It was in a little Irish pub that I heard it, that song that made such a difference in my life. Gus O'Connor's Pub, it was. In Doolin, County Clare. The remote west of Ireland. So remote, and so clinging to the very edge of the Atlantic, that locals call America "the next parish west."

I had gone there—well, sort of escaping. Here's the story: I had been President of William Jewell College about five years, and I felt we were ready to take some big steps toward becoming not just a good college but one of the very best in America. We were going to soar, to swoop, to sail, to "mount up with wings as eagles."

Then, all of a sudden, it all unraveled, through some circumstances none of us could control, so that now instead of soaring and swooping and sailing I was looking up to see bottom. Dashed. Bewildered. Didn't know exactly what to do next. You know what I mean—you may have been there. So I decided to go away for awhile and think it all out—psychologists call it "flight," and of course it was a literal flight on a very real Aer Lingus plane—and I found myself in Ireland, in this little village, and in this little pub, listening to three young Irishmen singing "The Garden Song."

(For a long time I thought it was an Irish tune with Irish words. But then I learned it had been written by an American, David Mallett, and was in fact a feature of children's programs like Captain Kangaroo, was sung by John Denver and Arlo Guthrie and who knows who else.) Whatever. It changed my life. And so I shared it in Opening Convocation once at William Jewell College, then with generations of Harlaxton students, semester by semester. I would sing it (and I can't sing a lick), students and faculty members would play guitars or other instruments as a kind of band, I would lead the whole College in singing it—several times—and sometimes it even became a song that we would sing through the semester and when students were leaving at end of term.

Here are the words—not all of them, but the ones we sang:

Inch by inch, and row by row,
We're gonna make this garden grow.
All it takes is a rake and a hoe
And a piece of fertile ground.

Inch by inch, and row by row,
Someone bless these seeds I sow.
Someone warm them from below
'Til the rains come tumbling down.

What that song said to me in that difficult time, in Gus O'Connor's Pub in Doolin, County Clare, Republic of Ireland, was what I said to Harlaxton students every semester, on their first or second day at Harlaxton Manor. And it went something like this:

1. At Harlaxton, **we work**.

(Inch by inch, and row by row / We're gonna make this garden grow. / All it takes is a rake and a hoe . . .)

"Academics are Job One. Our libraries and labs are our rakes and hoes, and they are at hand 24/7. Our library never closes, our minds never close. We **work** at getting a good education. Whatever else is happening, we **work** at our studies."

2. At Harlaxton, **we are grateful** for the gifts that are given us, and we use those gifts to do good and worthy things.

(Inch by inch, and row by row / . . . All it takes is . . . a piece of fertile ground.)

Our "fertile ground" is our God-given gifts and talents — the gifts of our skills and abilities, the gifts of our intelligence, the gifts of love and care from family and friends, the gifts of good teachers, the gift of our mind-blowing opportunity to be at Harlaxton.

3. At Harlaxton, **we depend on powers that are larger than we are,** powers that help us and see us through, that help us achieve what we thought impossible.

(Inch by inch, and row by row / Someone bless these seeds I sow. / Someone warm them from below / 'Til the rains come tumbling down.)

> We can't send the rains. We can't warm the seeds from deep within the earth. We can't do "impossible" things on our own. And so we depend on our God, on our care and support for one another, on the spirit of "Yes" that pervades Harlaxton. And these powers that are larger than ourselves help us achieve beyond our highest dreams.

I don't know if anyone else got all of that meaning out of that simple little song, but we surely sang it with zest and joy. It had made, it still makes, a great difference in my own life and work. I hope it did, and does, for others. I saw it happen: I went back to William Jewell, and we all *worked* hard together, and we used the *gifts* given us, and we *depended on God* and on each other and on powers bigger than any of us, and we created together some very fine years in a very fine college. Same during some good years at Health Midwest. Same at Harlaxton.

It's important, sometimes, what a little song can do. Even if you don't hear it in church, or in school, but in a pub.

Gus O'Connor's Pub.

Doolin.

County Clare.

Republic of Ireland.

Where America is "the next parish west."

"Did You Get To Travel?"

Ah, that's the question from fellow students back home.

As I say in another of these sketches, Harlaxton students consistently told us — when we asked them — that their prime goal in coming to Harlaxton was to travel, though they also wanted to master their classwork and keep their Grade Point Averages high. A substantial number of them worried that the tough Harlaxton academic program might keep them from traveling as much as they wanted to do.

But Harlaxton also fosters a strong degree of independence, and students learned to manage their time so that travel and studies could *both* be achieved. The Harlaxton program itself helps, in that our British and American faculties don't fight the travel urge, but instead co-opt it and make it a part of the learning in British Studies and in many other courses. We even had funds from some fine donors in America that helped students who couldn't otherwise have experienced this important learning through travel.

So, away our students went, every weekend. I cite in another sketch a November weekend chosen at random, when students traveled to Paris, Barcelona, Athens, London, Amsterdam, Prague, Oxford, Berlin, Inverness, Lille, Zermatt, Leeds, Ireland, Edinburgh, Copenhagen, Rome, Interlaken, Iceland, Lyon, Tuscany, York, Stratford, Stockholm, Cambridge. All this on one weekend!

This is pretty good exposure to the wider world for students from Eau Claire, WI or Charleston, IL or Evansville, IN or Seguin, TX or Baldwin City, KS or Bowling Green, KY or Denton, TX!

So, the answer to the students back home is a rousing "Yes, we traveled! Did we ever travel! And was it ever good!"

Strangely enough, now that we are back in America, people sometimes ask the same question of us "grown up" folks. "I know you were leading the whole college," they say. "And," with a nod to Suzanne, "I know you were working hard all the time to make Harlaxton a better place for students and faculty and guests. All those things take a lot of time. But did you get to travel?"

And we smile.

Consider this, if you will: I used to help students understand how close British and European cities were from Harlaxton Manor by telling them that I used to walk out the door of our house in the Kansas City suburb of Lee's Summit, MO, travel three and a half hours, and be in St. Louis. Whereas at Harlaxton, I could walk out the door of the Principal's Lodge, travel the same three and a half hours, and be in Paris. "Now," I would tell them, "I like St. Louis a lot, but . . .." And they would chant in chorus, "But it isn't Paris!" Right.

And so, as Suzanne says, "We were like the kids," traveling every chance we could get. In near-twelve years you get a lot of chances.

I can't even begin to list all the places we went: London, often, really whenever we wanted, because it was only seventy minutes away by fast train. Oxford and Cambridge, Coventry and Leicester, Bath and Edinburgh, Stonehenge and Salisbury, Canterbury and Hastings, Bury St. Edmunds and Norwich and York and Durham, Stratford upon Avon for the Royal Shakespeare Theatre, Wales and Ireland — lots of times to Ireland, Stamford and Nottingham and Lincoln. Paris every semester, Normandy and Chartres and Strasbourg and Toulouse and St. Jean Pied de Port, Brittany and the Loire Valley, Monet's Giverny and William the Conqueror's Caen. Rome and Florence and Venice, multiple times. Sicily, Tuscany, Lake Orta and Lake Maggiore, Switzerland and the Alps for Christmas. Berlin and Martin Luther's Wittenberg. Athens, Ithaca, Sparta, Thebes, Corinth, Thessalonica. Seville in beautiful Spain. Driving up Mt. Olympus and climbing up Mt. Sinai — and coming down again. Crete and the early Minoan civilization at Knossos. Egypt and the Nile, Alexandria and Cairo. Israel and Jordan. Couldn't get to Ancient Carthage because Libya kept acting up, or to Croatia because of constant conflicts. And other places I don't remember. Yes, we got to travel. Big time! And it was part of the life-enriching, life-changing experience of the years at Harlaxton.

But, somehow, we never got to Skegness, that holiday center ("centre") on the North Sea where a lot of Brits congregate to ride donkeys on the beach and eat fish and chips and buy cotton candy and watch their white skins turn blue in the cold ocean water before turning red with sunburn when the sun comes out. Sound charming? It is only ninety minutes from Grantham by train.

I always wanted to go to Skegness, but somehow never made it.

Guest we'll just have to go back again and finish the travels.

Selfie Sin?

Smile! Click!

Look! That's ME in front of the Colosseum!
Look! That's ME in front of the Eiffel Tower!
Look! That's ME in front of Harlaxton Manor!
Look! That's ME in front of Big Ben!
Look! That's ME, That's ME, That's ME, That's ME, That's ME, That's ME.
Oh, and Look Here, Too! That's also ME.

Lotta good pictures messed up by the ME.

Don't get me wrong: nothing wrong with a Selfie. (Grin and Click!)

It is a superb form of documentation for some brilliant travels. We can show — to ourselves and to others — that we were really there, that we experienced "this wonderful place and all that it means." And we can do it instantly: Mom or Boyfriend in Paducah gets the image almost as soon as it happens.

But if we do it right, both *before* and *after* the Selfie and the Smile there is the digging, the reading, the learning, the discovering, the embracing, the knowing about and experiencing "this wonderful place and all that it means."

The Selfie says, "I was here."

It takes a good bit more to be able to say, "It *mattered* that I was here."

And that's the difference between a Tourist and a Traveller.

For the Tourist it's all about ME: it is all Selfies, as in Selfish, as in Self-centered. The place doesn't really matter, except as a stage set for ME. More important, the people of the place, their history and their struggles, their stories and their cares don't matter either. It is still all about ME: The Original Sin.

For the Traveller, on the other hand, it is all about Discovering, Learning, Doing, about Knowing and Shaping and Improving the world we find. There is Adventure and Exploration in it, and this is good. There is Excitement and Energy, Learning and Personal Growth. And at the end of our journeys, there is, and we have, a resolve to leave it all better than we found it—whether it is a place, a person, a life, a world.

That's why Harlaxton seeks to turn Tourists into Travelers.

Look! The Colosseum!

A Hero at the Security Desk?

Yup.

That's right.

That familiar face at that familiar Security and Assistance Desk at little old Harlaxton College belongs to Doug Mitchell. There he is — looking after the kids, looking after the Manor and its grounds all through the night, keeping everything safe and under control, greeting guests and checking them in with a warm welcome.

Few people know that he is also a decorated hero with Her Majesty's Special Forces.

They know other things about him. They know, for example, that he speaks with a Scottish brogue. They know he smiles a lot, laughs with a big laugh, gets his job done just like it should be done.

Some Harlaxton alums, from earlier days, will remember him as a driver, taking them in and out of Grantham in his "Scottish Shuttle Bus," the blue and white banner of St. Andrew hanging just inside his front "windscreen" — just to be clear about an important fact in his life. And are there any questions?

People may sense subliminally that he is courageous, even fearless, that he probably doesn't take any guff. Or any nonsense, humbug, blather, blither, bosh, bull, bunk, claptrap, crapola, drivel, flapdoodle, folderol, garbage, hogwash, hokum, horsefeathers, moonshine, muck, rot, poppycock, rubbish, tommyrot, trash, trumpery, or twaddle, either. He just does his job, with a certain strength and firmness.

"Strength and firmness." Ah, there you have the story.

For Doug Mitchell grew up on the Scottish Borders, at Berwick-upon-Tweed, just a giant's stone's throw from the Holy Island of Lindisfarne. At age "17 years and 3 months" he enlisted in the King's Own Scottish Borderers Regiment, being shipped out after basic training—as part of The Lowland Brigade—to Germany, where the Iron Curtain had descended and Cold War relations with the Soviet Union were tense at best. After eighteen months he applied for and was accepted into Her Majesty's Special Forces, a special ops organization of Britain's elite fighting men. Think Army Rangers. Think Navy Seals. Think Marine Recon. Think Green Berets. For thirteen years he saw duty in the hottest trouble spots of the world: Borneo, Malaya, Kuwait, the United Arab Emirates, and Northern Ireland, among others. His operations were often secret, his heroism often unreported.

For he was, and is, a true hero. In Borneo, on one occasion, he picked up a wounded comrade, carried him on his back through jungle and swamp, fighting his way to a remote jungle base and a relative, momentary safety. In Scotland he saved a group of school children crossing a road by grabbing the steering wheel of an army truck, the driver having collapsed over the wheel, and with great strength of muscle and will crashing that truck into a stone wall instead of into the children. On another occasion, acting by his own moral compass instead of the misguidance of British Intelligence, he saved an Irish family, a father, mother, and two children, from being murdered by his own Special Forces unit.

He was busted in rank for this latter operation, though later reinstated. Overall, in his thirteen years with the Special Forces, he became a much-decorated soldier with a chest full of medals. List them and count them:

The Military Cross, for "an act or acts of exemplary gallantry during active operations against the enemy on land";

The Military Medal, for "acts of gallantry and devotion to duty under fire";

The Queen's Gallantry Medal, for "exemplary acts of bravery";

The Queen's Commendation for Bravery, for "gallantry entailing risk to life and meriting national recognition";

The Borneo Medal, for "campaign service in [the dangers of] Borneo";

The Northern Ireland Medal, for "campaign service in [the dangers of] Northern Ireland."

After his military career, Doug was a policeman with the Northumberland and then the West Yorkshire units, then in private transport security with TNT and Chubb. And then to Harlaxton.

Just a year or so ago Doug's daughter Victoria, part as a whimsy and part in seriousness, purchased as a gift for Doug a bit of Scottish land in the Highlands that carried with it the title Lord Douglas Mitchell of Glencoe. I don't know if she knew at the time that Glencoe was the site of an infamous massacre of 1692 (in Scottish Gaelic called *Mort Ghlinne Comhann*, or Murder of Glen Coe) when members of Clan MacDonald were treacherously murdered by members of Clan Campbell who had accepted their hospitality — all in a squabble over whether Catholic King James or Protestant King William should be on the throne. British Studies students would know about King William and King James.

As I say, when Doug came to Harlaxton, and since, not many people knew or have known of his distinguished and heroic service to his country and, it being Britain, to the Crown. He is just "Doug," doing his job. Though one evening, late at night, when a student had been drinking too much and was being especially mouthy, I heard another guy quiet him down instantly by pointing to Doug and whispering, "See that Security man over there? He served in Her Majesty's Special Forces — he's killed people!" Sobers a drunk up pretty fast.

As every student and alum of the last twenty years knows, there is an important lecture in British Studies on "Britain and Ireland," focusing on "The Troubles" in strife-ridden Northern Ireland, where Doug Mitchell served and was decorated. As Principal, I thought one year that it would be very good for our students if I asked Doug to speak from his own experiences in Northern Ireland, to tell his own story in his own words, in a gathering just before dinner, at 5:00 in Schroeder Lounge, for any who wanted to come. It wasn't required or even expected, but just an opportunity to hear from a soldier who had "been there." Maybe it could give a human face of personal experience to that morning's academic lecture. I had myself presented that lecture at one time and knew how difficult it was to make the struggles, the killings, the bombings "real" to our American students who had never experienced such.

I'm not sure that our British Studies Faculty approved—they did not attend, and one of my very finest colleagues and friends finally said, "I guess it is all right having Doug do this, so long as students know it is one person's experience and opinion." Which pretty much describes, as I observed in response, just about any class presentation at any time, as all but the most naïve students fully understand.

So Doug spoke, to the 40-to-50 interested souls who showed up, standing up there on his feet in a corner of Schroeder Lounge (remember, he earned his medals not as a lecturer, not as a speaker, but as a warrior), looking at all of us who had come to listen, remembering deep and hidden things he had known, and then just releasing them, telling us, in a matter-of-fact way, his personal experiences of life and death, including his own life, and his own times of being near death—not dramatizing them, but just telling them, and keeping the audience riveted by the intensity of what took place, what he had to do and chose to do in some critical moments of the Irish story. Big strong Doug wept a couple of times during his talk, and he told me later that it was the first time he had talked about these things—which made me feel bad about asking him until he assured me that it had been good for him to let them out of his soul. He did this informal talk maybe three times in three different semesters, then said he probably shouldn't do it any more. I was sorry he felt he had to quit, though I certainly understood.

At the very end of his first time, his first talk, just as he was ending, Doug Mitchell grew quiet, for what seemed like a long time. He kept looking around at all of us, university people from across America, all of us caught up in the drama of what he had been saying, the "real life" quality of it all, and he just stood there silent, until I was a little worried for him. And then as if it were wrenching itself from his deepest soul, he said, "I need to say this before I stop talking: there is very little difference between being a hero and being stupid."

Seldom does one get such honesty.

And I thought, "All of us are stupid from time to time.

"But few of us are ever heroes."

Doug Mitchell was a hero, is a hero. "Strength and firmness." And no one can take that away.

So here's to Lord Douglas Mitchell of Glencoe. Security and Assistance man at Harlaxton College.

And Hero.

"At the Eleventh Hour, of the Eleventh Day, of the Eleventh Month . . ."

Britain Remembers!

All of Britain Remembers!

O, yes, we have our Veterans' Day in America, and we honor the men and women who have served our country. With public statements and great hurrahs, with dramatic and deep-voiced introductions at sporting events, with flags on every wall, with soul-stirring and family-loving images on television (though I notice that these bleed over very quickly and not so subtly into ads for insurance or beer), we pay our tributes. It is right that we do so.

But it is somehow different in Britain. In America, we tend to scream and clap and cheer our remembrances. In Britain, we were quiet, reverent, even prayerful.

Perhaps part of this is owing to the huge suffering Britain knew in two world wars, their terrible loss of life. America suffered greatly, also, especially in World War II, though not on our own soil. But we have never known anything even approximating the British loss in World War I, when a whole generation of young men died in the trenches of Europe, a whole generation of parents lost their sons, a whole generation of young women lost husbands and lovers. In the midst of this great pain, Britain learned Remembrance, connecting it ceremonially to that moment when the World War I Armistice was signed—11:00am on November 11, 1918—that is (as it is usually intoned, rhythmically and slowly and reverently, with ceremonial pauses), at "the Eleventh Hour . . . of the Eleventh Day . . . of the Eleventh Month."

Harlaxton has also known war, and wars. Armed bands of marauders in the 1300s when John of Gaunt no doubt stayed at the first Harlaxton Manor, a hunting lodge in Harlaxton Village. The place had a moat around it, and moats are not for friends. Or the Wars of Religion in Europe of the 1500s and 1600s, when French rulers were killing Protestants — in a complicated way connecting to the purchase of the Harlaxton estates by the wealthy Protestant Daniel DeLigne in 1619.* Or there was that unpleasantness in 1776 when the British troops at Lexington and Concord, then at Bunker Hill, were country lads from Lincolnshire, from the villages around Harlaxton. All this was related to the "old" Harlaxton Manor, in Harlaxton Village.

Now fast forward to "new" Harlaxton, the one we know and love. During World War I the "Harlaxton Aerodrome" was created out back of the Manor, a large training base for young men learning to fly those dangerous Sopwith Camel canvas biplanes for the Royal Flying Corps. Out front, where farm fields are now planted, replicas of German and British trenches were dug, as were pits for the new and deadly technology of the machine gun, and behold, Harlaxton became a trench warfare school as well as an army flying school.** The son of Harlaxton Manor's "squire," Philip Pearson Gregory, was not exempt: he went off to war as an officer in the Grenadier Guards, was wounded in the horrible battle of Passchendaele in 1917, and received Britain's second highest award for bravery, the Military Cross. Harlaxton fields now had a different kind of crop.

Just twenty years later, World War II again called Harlaxton Manor into service, ultimately as headquarters for the First British Airborne Division, the place where these brave paratroopers trained for D-Day. They were held in reserve on D-Day, but shortly after were sent on a supremely dangerous mission, an attack on a strategic bridge at Arnhem, in Holland. It was, as the books and films have dramatized, "A Bridge Too Far," for they landed in the teeth of a German panzer division unknown to British intelligence. They suffered an 80% casualty rate: of every five young men who went out from Harlaxton Manor, only one came back — a huge sacrifice of young lives for their country, and for our present freedoms.

Their residence at Harlaxton led to construction of the Pegasus Monument in the courtyard that now bears its name — Pegasus, the divine Flying Horse of Greek legend, being their emblem. Harlaxton has preserved it over the years.

And so in 2009 we invited Parachute Regimental veterans back to Harlaxton to relive and to remember. The words below were a portion of the welcome I gave them in a ceremony in our Long Gallery, with actor Richard Todd, himself a veteran of the Regiment, headlining the program:

> So, today, the honored members of the Parachute Regiment bring the Airborne back "Home" to Harlaxton Manor. Here the First Airborne planned and dreamed, here they laughed and cried, here they slept and ate, from here these brave souls went out to defend the treasured freedoms of free peoples, including those of us in both England and America who make up what Mr. Churchill called "the English speaking race." Of the many who went out from Harlaxton Manor, only a few returned. It is fitting that we remember them on this day.

Year after year, these veterans, old and growing older, would return to conduct a "Remembrance Ceremony" at the Pegasus Monument. Smart in their blue blazers and maroon berets, chests bedecked with their numerous medals, the veterans would approach the Monument, our students and our staff would gather around, some of our students would participate by planting little wooden crosses of remembrance into the ground next to the Monument, regimental flags and Union Jack would be presented and lowered, the bugle would sound "The Last Post" — its haunting strains drifting over all of Harlaxton Manor. And then, together with these wizened former paratroopers, we would say Britain's ritual words of memorial to all those who had fallen in defense of liberty:

> They shall grow not old, as we that are left grow old:
> Age shall not weary them, nor the years condemn.
> At the going down of the sun and in the morning,
> **We will remember them.**

For a few inspiring moments, we Americans of Harlaxton College walked hand-in-hand, step-by-step, with our British friends and colleagues, our British allies, in these important ceremonies of Remembrance. We learned that every year, at "the Eleventh Hour of the Eleventh Day of the Eleventh Month," these same words are said in services and ceremonies all across Britain — in churches, in village halls, in public spaces, on radio and television, everywhere in the land. And the people of Britain gather to Remember.

During the weeks before, these same people have been wearing symbolic "red poppies," as did we, remembering the blood that was shed in Flanders fields and in all conflicts where lives were lost in the defense of liberty. As we of Harlaxton College joined them, we felt not so foreign any longer, for we were standing together in our shared histories and our resolves and our hopes. At the sound of the bells at 11:00 o'clock, "the Eleventh Hour," all sounds would be stilled, for two full minutes of silent remembrance.

And then, at the end of the silence, heads bowed reverently, all of Britain would murmur together, and we of Harlaxton with them,

We will remember them.

*Engineering professor Dr. Mark Valenzuela of the University of Evansville, who loves Harlaxton College and is probably the world's authority on the heraldry in Harlaxton Manor, has researched the DeLigne connection extensively. In October 2015, his work on this complicated topic will be published in the *Huguenot Society Journal* (a publication of the Huguenot Society of Great Britain and Ireland).

**Dr. Edward Bujak, a very fine professor of Harlaxton's British Faculty, is researching Harlaxton's role in World War I. In Fall 2015, I. B. Tauris will publish his book entitled *Reckless Fellows: The Gentlemen of the Royal Flying Corps*. It tells "the remarkable story of the World War I pioneer pilots at Harlaxton Manor" and how trainees came from all over the world—Britain, Australia, New Zealand, South Africa, Canada, the United States—to become the world's first fighter-pilots and Harlaxton's first global citizens. In 2017, Bloomsbury Books will publish his *English Landed Society in the Great War*, a look at the impact of World War I on great estates like Harlaxton Manor, including the farms and cottages associated with these great estates.

The Wandering Scholar:
On Teaching at Harlaxton

It's a great gig. Except.

I'm talking about the Visiting Faculty, now, those nine or ten American profs who come for a semester from the home and partner campuses to teach courses in their own academic disciplines. They join the four members of the resident British Faculty to make up the group we always touted at Opening Convocation and Valedictory Dinner as "The Faculty of Harlaxton College."

These brave folks would apply for a Harlaxton teaching post at their own college or university, which would then nominate the successful applicants to Harlaxton. Their own school would pay their salaries, travel, and sometimes other faculty development stipends. Harlaxton would select from the nominees according to the needs of our curriculum, the housing we had available ('cause families came, too), and the degree of student participation from the nominee's campus.

Thus it was that every semester, just as with our student body so with our faculty, we were bringing together people from a wide variety of very different colleges, spread across America, and in one weekend turning them into "The Harlaxton Faculty." Amazingly, it worked.

As with Harlaxton students, it takes a certain heightened sense of imagination, of possibility, of flexibility, even of courage for a faculty member to come to Harlaxton, especially if children are involved. (In fact, the kids were my greatest heroes, for they didn't have any choice in the matter and in their English schools lacked the kind of support from American classmates that our college students had. Fortunately, the local schools were welcoming, as well as being very good.)

Just think about it: leaving house and home, leaving everything that is familiar, leaving friends and church and community and extended family, all to follow the romantic dream of teaching in an English manor house at the doorstep of all Europe. It's a big decision, a big set of tradeoffs. Some couldn't do it—couldn't leave their friends or the church or the gym or the dog.

But mostly it worked.

In many cases, it brought teachers back to their first love, the things that brought them into their profession in the first place: teaching their subject matter to good students, usually in small classes, with great support at every level. Add to that the opportunities for class and personal travel, for connections with English universities and scholars, for personal research and writing in the libraries of Oxford or Cambridge or Nottingham or London, and it all added up to a superb opportunity to grow professionally—for those who could see it and who would take advantage of it. Their home campuses would have called it "Faculty Development," and some of those campuses valued it as that.

On the personal side, lodgings and meals in Harlaxton Manor were provided at no cost: as a faculty spouse said about free meals for her family in the Refectory, "They are great meals. I don't do the shopping, I don't do the cooking, I don't do the cleaning up—they are great meals." As to the lodgings, they were beautiful state bedrooms or very convenient faculty "flats." Yes, a great gig.

Except. Except a room is not a house, and certainly not "my house," and it was not "my town" or "my school," and initially these were not "my friends."

A few teachers struggled in this setting. Most thrived. Members of some faculty groups formed close friendships and did lots of things together, based out of their splendid Senior Common Room (the Van der Elst Room, the one room in the Manor that was "faculty only"). In other semesters, faculty persons tended to do as the students and travel most weekends, doing their own thing.

All in all, as I say, it "worked" well for faculty as well as for students. They understood, down deep, that it was their teaching that mattered most, and they did their jobs "well and faithfully."

I once asked faculty members for "a sentence" about teaching at Harlaxton, and Theatre Professor Patti McCrory of the University of Evansville said it as well anyone could ever, ever say it. It is, in fact, a kind of Harlaxton poetry:

> Let us be in a place where learning is valued every hour of the day and we are nurtured to do more than teach; a place that affords our students opportunities to know a vital theatre and to be among vital audiences who clamor for more; a place that gives us pause from the minutia of living and somehow connects us to the eternal, by way of traveling—or simply walking down the lane with the wind blowing at our backs; pausing to be, pausing to enjoy, pausing to think with a sigh, "Oh, this is Harlaxton."

The Tabula Is Rasa

I have long been fascinated with the "Freshman Mindset Lists" coming out of Beloit College each year. For one thing, they take seriously the notion that a teacher must start where his or her student "is at." For another, the Lists are simply stunning to teachers with any years in the profession—just the youth of their charges, and the things they have known and not known.

Then it happened somehow that, when we left Harlaxton, we moved to Beloit, Wisconsin, population 38,000, a town of nice diversity for the upper Midwest, with a greater racial mix than most towns in these parts, and a good mix of industry and agriculture (think cheese and dairy), and—ta da—lovely little Beloit College, home of the "Lists." And of Tom McBride and Ron Nieff, current and former Beloit faculty/staff members who create the "Lists" each year, and who have given their permission and even their blessing for my use of this particular "List," © Beloit College.

I've met Tom and Ron, have lunched and chatted with Ron, and I guess they are as surprised as any of us at what their analyses show. But they are right to take the data seriously, I think, both as educators and as oracles of America's "pop culture."

This all got me to thinking, of course, about the students coming into Harlaxton each fall and spring.

Just a sample: the kids at Harlaxton this year (2014-15) were generally born in 1994 or 1995. That's as in 1994 and 1995. That's pretty young to most stodgy professors of thirty or above!

And here's a profile of them, from the Beloit College Mindset Lists:

> When they arrive on campus, these digital natives are already well connected to each other.
> They are more likely to have borrowed money for college than their Boomer parents were, and while their parents foresee four years of school, the students are pretty sure it will be longer than that.

Members of this year's first year class, most of them born in 1995, will search for the academic majors reported to lead to good-paying jobs, and most of them will take a few courses taught at a distant university by a professor they will never meet.

The use of smart phones in class may indicate they are reading the assignment they should have read last night, or they may be recording every minute of their college experience — or they may be texting the person next to them.

If they are admirers of Steve Jobs and Bill Gates, they may wonder whether a college degree is all it's cracked up to be, even as their dreams are tempered by the reality that tech geniuses come along about as often as Halley's Comet, which they will not glimpse until they reach what we currently consider "retirement age."

Though they have never had the chicken pox, they are glad to have access to health insurance for a few more years.

They will study hard, learn a good deal more, teach their professors quite a lot, and realize eventually that they will soon be in power. After all, by the time they hit their thirties, four out of ten voters will be of their generation. Whatever their employers may think of them, politicians will be paying close attention.

For this generation of entering college students, Dean Martin, Mickey Mantle, and Jerry Garcia have always been dead.

They are the sharing generation, having shown tendencies to share everything, including possessions, no matter how personal.

For them, "GM" means food that is Genetically Modified.

As they started to crawl, so did the news across the bottom of the television screen.

"Dude" has never had a negative tone.

Having a chat has seldom involved talking.

Gaga has never been baby talk.

They could always get rid of their outdated toys on eBay.

They have known only two presidents.

Their TV screens keep getting smaller as their parents' screens grow ever larger.

PayPal has replaced a pen pal as a best friend on line.

Rites of passage have more to do with having their own cell

phone and Skype accounts than with getting a driver's license and car.

The U.S. has always been trying to figure out which side to back in Middle East conflicts.

A tablet is no longer something you take in the morning.

Plasma has never been just a bodily fluid.

The Pentagon and Congress have always been shocked, absolutely shocked, by reports of sexual harassment and assault in the military.

With GPS, they have never needed directions to get someplace, just an address.

Java has never been just a cup of coffee.

Americans and Russians have always cooperated better in orbit than on earth.

Their parents have always bemoaned the passing of precocious little Calvin and sarcastic stuffy Hobbes.

The U.S. has always imposed economic sanctions against Iran.

They have never attended a concert in a smoke-filled arena.

As they slept safely in their cribs, the Oklahoma City bomber and the Unabomber were doing their deadly work.

They have never really needed to go to their friend's house so they could study together.

Kevin Bacon has always maintained six degrees of separation in the cinematic universe.

They may have been introduced to video games with a new Sony PlayStation left in their cribs by their moms.

They have always been able to plug into USB ports.

Their parents' car CD player is soooooo ancient and embarrassing.

They have always known that there are "five hundred, twenty five thousand, six hundred minutes" in a year.

Wow! And Whew! What does all this say to me?

That the Tabula is *indeed* Rasa.

But whose Tabula?

And which Rasa?

Brick Cheesecake:
A Meet a Family Saga

It all started with the greatest of hopes!

David and Janet Armes, stalwart leaders of the Harlaxton Meet a Family Programme for more than thirty years, had invited "their" three or four students once again to their home at Moat House in Harlaxton Village (right next door to the gates of the original Harlaxton manor house, until Gregory Gregory moved it and built "our" manor house in the 1830s). And — drum roll — on this visit the students were going to cook a meal for *them*, their English Mum and Dad, instead of the other way 'round. *A real American meal.*

The excitement was palpable. "Rick" — that's the name I'll give him, in order to protect the guilty (and besides I don't know who it was, by name) had phoned his mother in America and got her never-fail recipe for the family's sure-hit holiday specialty, Molasses-based Cheesecake. Yum.

There was, to be sure, a problem: no molasses in Britain. But Rick was a Harlaxton student and not to be deterred. He asked around, did a little research, and learned that "molasses" in America is "treacle" in England. Problem solved.

So Rick and his friends went to ASDA (the British Walmart), Rick bought a "tin of treacle" and as "Dad" David Armes tells the story, Rick then combined the proper ingredients and waited for the delicious American cheesecake to "set."

It did.

Set solid.

Like a brick.

Dismay all around. Rick is momentarily crushed. What could possibly have gone wrong? And, mentally retracing the steps, all blame it on the suspicious "tin of treacle," obviously a different product from what it would have been if it were molasses from an American store.

"Not to be thwarted," David Armes still speaking, "I went to our garage and from our car got a cold chisel and a hammer. We cleaned the tools good. Then we 'applied' them to the 'cheesecake,' breaking it apart and then eating it—slowly, so as not to break a tooth or two. Actually it wasn't too bad. And what a laugh and what a good evening we had."

There must be a hundred, a thousand stories like this from the three decades of Meet a Family, with British hosts bringing Harlaxton students (and faculty members) into their homes, and also sometimes taking them out to restaurants and sporting events and the theatre, giving them a further touch of "real England."

Lifetime friendships have been formed through this program, with American students bringing their American parents to meet their "British parents," and with British Mums and Dads going to graduations, weddings, and christenings in America. I do know that when American alums return to Harlaxton, they first receive the Manor's warm embrace, then hotfoot it to see their Meet a Family Mums and Dads—even if it was ten, fifteen years ago. And I remember one couple from the Harlaxton Village, Michael and Margaret Laws, spending a whole month in America, beginning in Denton, Texas, and ending up in Eau Claire, Wisconsin, visiting with their former Meet a Family students at every stop along the way! (For British readers, that's about as far as you can go from south to north in the central United States—from near-Mexico to near-Canada, a distance of more than a thousand miles!)

"The Meet a Family Programme" formally began in 1982-83 with the Grantham Rotary Club, of which David Armes was and is a member. As the Club moved on to other projects, David and Janet continued to lead an active program of family hosting that, because it is a good thing, sort of took on a life of its own. The College provides some staff support, but it remains a volunteer program.

And what lovely volunteers!

During our years at Harlaxton, David briefed new students each semester, in the Long Gallery, on what to expect in a British family home. Someone along the way had given him an American baseball cap, red, which he would bring to the briefing, plopping it on his full head of ever-so-handsome white hair, turning it around backwards to be "cool," then explaining that you don't wear a cap or hat inside your host family's home. He gave some "Do's" and "Don'ts," an essential list of basic courtesy: do keep appointments, do keep in touch with your family, do write thank you notes, do offer a little gift at first and last meetings, do be on time, don't smoke in your hosts' home, do offer to help out, do offer to buy a round of drinks if taken to a pub, don't take your dirty laundry to be washed at your Meet a Family home (it actually happened once — only once). David was charming with the students, didn't rant or talk down to them, and they "got it."

It was, and is, truly a great program. David and Janet are great leaders. And Harlaxton students consistently rank this experience as #1 or #2 in their time abroad.

So, when I grow up, I want to go back to Harlaxton and have my very own Meet a Family hosts. And I will *always* say "Thank You," and I will *never* smoke or bring dirty laundry with me.

And I've got this killer recipe for Borscht Cheesecake that I'd like to try . . . .

"Glo"

She is a force of nature. And we could see it, sense it, feel it at once.

"Glo" — Gloria Atanmo — came to Harlaxton from Baker University in the Fall semester of 2012. Immediately, we could see that she was "different." Somehow larger than life, communicating an infectious enthusiasm, a leader to her classmates, she was not afraid to say what a privilege it is to be at Harlaxton, what a privilege we have to be Americans ("God bless 'merica"), what a great country Britain is ("God Save the Queen"), and how it is cool to show enthusiasms for the things that matter.

A great athlete and gifted leader, she was also greatly talented in media and advertising, having had her own PR business back home in Baldwin City, Kansas. By the force of her person and the skill of her promotion, she rallied Harlaxton to good causes throughout her semester. In a sense, she put Harlaxton into a multi-colored media box for all of us and helped us see better what we were holding, what was holding us.

If things got dark, "Glo" brought light. If things got confused, "Glo" simplified and unraveled. If people were down, "Glo" picked them up. If people were self-centered and complaining, "Glo" reminded us of who we were and where we were and what great privileges we were sharing, what great experiences we were having. She made the long, dark English days brighter, not in a shallow way, but with the force of truth and hope.

After she had gone back to Baker and finished her degree, we asked her to return to Harlaxton as an Intern, and for another semester she worked her magic all through Harlaxton College.

Last time I was in touch with her, "Glo" was in Barcelona, playing semi-professional basketball, teaching English, no doubt doing her media stuff, and drinking in a whole new culture. I asked her for advice in finishing off these sketches about Harlaxton — on the tech stuff, telling her I am a technological dunce on two continents. I did *not* ask her what Harlaxton had meant to her, but she spoke out for herself, saying that Harlaxton College changed her in a way that no other experience could. Her way of framing the familiar "Harlaxton changed my life"?

Thing is, she is *acting* on it in an extraordinary way. Because now, at this time in her life, she has resolved to live "for the mystery, adventure, and growth that comes with traveling and discovering new cultures." She has "left my footprints in fifteen countries so far," and she is determined that she won't stop traveling until she has lived in every continent of the world and "breathed the oxygen of the many vibrant and dynamic cultures around us."

So far . . . it's gone well. Different cultures, hard times, humbling moments, but still the sense that "living out of a suitcase, both literally and metaphorically—equipped with my carry-on luggage of taking risks and keeping a positive spirit—are my current destiny. I want to learn every day, and I also want to inspire and teach the hundreds of people I am meeting. There's no turning back."

So let me go back to her first days at Harlaxton, where Gloria was not only a force of nature but also a force for good, for all of us. I'm sure that in Barcelona as well, and wherever she may go in this wide wide world, Gloria will make all those around her better people.

It's just who she is.

She's "Glo."*

*You can find Glo at **www.TheBlogAbroad.com**. Her e-mail address and signature are fascinating to me: **globetrottingglo@---.com**, and she signs herself "Gloria Atanmo. Globetrotter| Photographer| Professional Risk Taker." It is not part of her e-mail signature, but perhaps it should be, for it is a tag line worthy of the most seasoned media guru: "Expensive dreams with an affordable hustle."

Diversity

So, some office at the home campus sent me a form letter asking for a report on "Diversity at Harlaxton."

I knew what they meant. I also knew how much easier it is to send a form letter than to answer it.

What they meant was "how many people of color ("colour") do you have enrolled?" What they really meant, mostly, related to enrollments of African Americans. A bit complicated, of course, because Harlaxton exists in, indeed is immersed in, the United Kingdom, where "diversity" most often refers to "Asians," by which is usually meant "Indians" (like, people from India) or Pakistanis. And where there is no such adjective or noun as "African British."

Yes, complicated.

A dutiful bureaucrat, I began to shape a response. I began with what I knew their internationally-blinkered little eyes were looking for back there in Vanderburgh County, Indiana, reporting quite honestly that our number of African Americans (though "Blacks" was more accurate, since several of our students were from Africa by way of American universities and were still citizens of their home countries) reflected the percentages on our home campus and Partner Colleges, and that our number of Hispanics was higher than the norm at American colleges (thanks chiefly to some wonderful young women coming from Texas Woman's University, our Partner school in Denton, TX).

I then moved to a description of our all-British staff—but British as in modern, multi-cultural Britain, with staff members coming from nearby towns and villages such as Grantham and Woolsthorpe-by-Belvoir and Croxton Kerrial, some born and raised there, but others having emigrated from exotic places like South Africa and Mozambique. (I never got it done, but we could have had some fine multi-cultural seminars for our students with just our food service and housekeeping staff members telling their personal stories, our students telling theirs, and then cutting loose with the lively discussion that would follow.)

Job Done. Report Ready to Send.

And no doubt it would have been satisfying and satisfactory to the folks sending out that form letter from that office back home in America. And to the government agency that asked for it. And to the Congress that required it.

But we hadn't even touched the surface of what diversity at Harlaxton was really all about. **And so I kept writing.**

For in Britain, the stunning fact was that **we were the minority**. We courteous and friendly and proud and energetic Americans, who charmed the British by our accents and "get it done" attitudes, who were accustomed to ruling the world, were a minority "race" in British culture.

Because we look so much like Brits and share a language (sort of) and much of a common history, because we have a "special relationship" and have fought and died together against totalitarian forces, people (including ourselves) are deluded into thinking we are two peas in a pod. But, no, my dear. We are two separate pods, and we produce quite different veggies. (And there I've gone and done it again, for the adjective "quite" is a real stumbling block, in America meaning "very much," "superlative," and in Britain often meaning "mediocre, a bit less than.")

It goes beyond driving on different sides of the road, or calling four-lane highways "dual carriageways" (which I still find charming). It goes beyond taking care to offer a person a "lift" instead of a "ride," the word "ride" meaning something a bit more personal than going somewhere in a car. Language can trip us up anywhere. But the fact is, any minority group experiences at least subtle discrimination, and that is true of Americans in Britain (and British people in America)—whether it be on immigration, or taxation, or just a general view of who knows what. A "minority," not by definition but almost always by practice, is seen as inferior, less than, not as good as.

We—the distinguished Principal and Spouse of Harlaxton College—were one evening standing on the great stone entry staircase of Harlaxton Manor, having already been residents of the Manor for more than ten years and feeling that we knew this great house very well We were wearing nice clothes and nice smiles, greeting British guests at a dignified function.

It all went well until one particularly officious woman guest began chiding us, severely and publicly—right there in the receiving line—for ignoring a room upstairs "that needs serious work." Now the fact of the matter was that Suzanne and our staff had totally repaired, restored, refurbished, and renewed that room, making it now one of the more attractive in the Manor. And so with quiet calm and genuine grace Suzanne explained those facts to the guest.

The response? "No, we were here for a concert four years ago, and that room needs serious work." Translation? You Americans can't possibly know anything about anything in Britain. Further translation? You are in a minority group, and you are therefore inferior in every way, including knowledge of your own house and your own work. Incredible, but real.

Now the guest probably meant no harm—she was just an unctuous wench, a "one off"—whereas the large majority of British people are unfailingly courteous and friendly. I hope we Americans are courteous as well, especially to the British people who come to our country. But the hard starchiness of her presumed superiority nearly split the stones we were standing on.

I am not here talking about British people or American people, about superiority or inferiority. I am talking about the dynamics of being in the minority, and the inescapable assumption that being in the minority means being somehow inferior.

I have no solution to offer except, "Get used to it" if you are to be in any "foreign" country. It can be a shock, but it is good for most white Americans to taste some of that experience. It might help us see and be more sensitive to the ways we treat other people. It may itself be one of the good things about coming to Harlaxton, for a student or for a faculty family. Yes, "Get used to it."

I never, by the way, heard back from that office in Evansville, Indiana, that had asked for the report, even though I met the deadline and sent a report that was clearly more involved than, and I hope more instructive than, a routine "checking ('ticking') the boxes." I would guess that this take on "Diversity" didn't fit the even bigger report in the sky that they were required to prepare. Didn't fit the categories. Couldn't find a way to squeeze this kind of talk into those tiny little blanks and squares.

But I didn't care.

I was just a member of a minority group over there in England.

What could I know!

Cars

They aren't.

Students don't have cars at Harlaxton.

There's no rule against it, that I know of. And years ago, when students tended to stay for a whole year and public transport* may have been a bit less convenient, some students would buy an old wreck and nurse it through their Harlaxton days. But not now.

Why is this, when we all know it is the goal of every fifteen-year-old American to drive at sixteen and own a car at sixteen and a half and drive to the moon at seventeen? When the gods of the young have either Wheels or a Screen or both, why this lack of interest in having a car at Harlaxton?

It makes sense, I guess. Public transport is fabulous in Britain, and in Europe generally. It is very easy to get around, anywhere. Harlaxton runs a shuttle bus to Grantham Town for connections to the world, several times every day, with Street Cars taxi taking up any slack.

You can't drive a car straight to Dublin or Paris or Rome—well, not without a ferryboat in between. Even our slowest students know Britain is an island. And why drive a car three hours to London, only to arrive in a city where gridlock makes it impossible to do anything but sit and smell exhaust fumes, when you can get there in one hour by train and have underground trains and buses to get you anywhere you want to go.

And so no cars.

Now, you wouldn't normally think about this, but just consider what a positive influence this is for good academics. Yes, most students are traveling most weekends, and to exotic places—though many, probably most, take their books with them when they go. But during the week?

No driving to a part-time job (and no part-time jobs), no driving home because they treat you nicer there, no driving just to drive, no traffic accidents, no driving while drinking. Being without a car tidies up one's schedule and finances, cuts out so many distractions, encourages a focus on the job at hand—to study, to learn.

I'm not against cars, though we didn't own one for nearly twelve years in Britain and were in for a series of shocks when we purchased our first suburban assault vehicle on returning to the States—sticker shock, size-of-car shock, entertainment-center-on-wheels shock, and a lovely cheap-petrol shock. But cars, a necessity in the USA, are less so in the UK; and not having one can take away a lot of clutter.

Having no car also takes away the problem of learning to drive on the "other" side of the road (not the "wrong" side, and understanding this simple language fact may be a first lesson in intercultural understanding). It takes away the need to master several linguistic usages: "windscreen" for "windshield," "boot" for "trunk," "tyre" for "tire, "box" for "muffler," "bonnet" for "hood," "petrol" for "gas," "dual carriageway" for "four-lane road," "motorway" for "interstate highway," "car park" for "parking lot," etc. etc. But this is small stuff: the real values are in the ability to focus on what is really important—studying—and in safety, for the driver and also for others.

Road safety is in fact *very* big in Britain. A person can't even *apply* for a driver's license until age seventeen, and laws are under consideration to make it eighteen. "Driving" license exams are very tough: (1) you send your passport off to Cardiff in Wales just to get permission to take a test (being sure in your heart you will never see that passport again); (2) then permission comes, and you are allowed to schedule a comprehensive test on the information in an extensive driver's manual. Part of this "theory" exam is a set of videos where you are to identify, with good reaction time, any developing driving hazards—like a truck about to pull out into your road, or a child chasing a ball. Trouble is, to an American, about anything that happens on a British road is a developing hazard, for roads are much narrower, road systems much more complicated, than in the USA. (3) If you pass both sections of this "theoretical" test, you can then proceed to schedule a "practical" exam, at a different time and place, a test you take with a driving examiner and which is much more than a formality—it is a serious, down and dirty examination of your fitness to drive on British roads. More trouble for the American: some things you are required to do, to be tested on, can be illegal in America—backing around a corner, for example. Or stopping in the middle of the road to turn the car around, a "three-point turn," they call it, right there in the middle of the road (mine were often fifty-two point turns). I would say to my driving instructor, "Jim, what if a truck just rams into us." He would say, "That's his problem." I would say, "Until he hits us—then it's our problem!" Or just pausing at a "Give Way" sign which in America would be a "Stop." Or learning to negotiate roundabouts. Most Brits, and certainly most Americans, take up to a year in driving lessons just to pass these tests.

As a consequence of all of this—the difficulty of these exams; the cost of cars and fuel, both heavily taxed, with petrol/gas costing about $8.50 per US gallon; and the ease of public transport, many people put off learning to drive in the UK, some of them forever.

Small wonder that our kids, there for only a semester, don't mess with cars. I was always glad they didn't. It made them better students, it kept them out of trouble, and it kept them alive.

*In Britain, "transportation" is used to describe the sending of prisoners to penal colonies in Australia or the U.S. State of Georgia in the eighteenth and nineteenth centuries, whereas "transport" means getting around by vehicle.

Professor Zyggy

He's a character like no other, is this Zygmund Dekanski.

From East London, he is, always the ethnic hotbed of The Metropolis. I once asked him if I could describe him as "Polish Cockney," and with that smile that lights up his lively eyes and his whole face and the whole world around him, Zyggy said "That's about right, Dawktor Kingsley."

(He always made "Doctor Kingsley" sound like a real person, maybe even a faintly decent person, whom Zyggy genuinely liked. I felt his warmth, as did everyone who knew him, and liked him immensely in return.)

He'd been around a bit, and in some interesting places. London, of course, and he had worked in Ireland, and he and his wife Merle had a property in France. But it was Harlaxton where he found a home, and where he helped make a home for others.

As to work assignment, Zyggy drove the shuttle bus. His title was Transport Coordinator, and he handled the "admin," the complicated, essential paper work and planning, quite well, thank you. But Zyggy drove the shuttle bus.

And he taught. The shuttle bus was his classroom, and he taught. He listened to students talking, and he probably knew more about Harlaxton students than did any other staff member, though he kept his counsel and their confidences. I don't remember, ever, his "ratting" to me about a single student, though I think he felt concern about many. And he would respond to students with good, practical, common sense, helping Harlaxton kids negotiate the shoals of British life and their new independence and their having to establish—and live—good priorities in an environment where "what the hell" was all too tempting.

Yes, Zyggy taught. A lot of us did the classroom stuff, which my colleagues carried out exceedingly well. Meanwhile, Zyggy taught life. And Zyggy taught good sense.

Sometimes Zyggy would get worked up, passionate, even angry. This was usually in a situation where he felt a colleague was being mistreated, or some wrong was being perpetrated or ignored, or some damn fool was acting like a damn fool. Then Zyggy, maybe frustrated that he couldn't make the "right" things happen, would grow quiet. I was always sad in these times and didn't quite know what to do. But the times didn't last, and Zyggy would quickly become, again, the one, the only, the incomparable, the irrepressible--ZYGGY. Professor Zyggy. Friend Zyggy.

As we were leaving Harlaxton for good, I created for Zyggy a certificate, something like the diplomas or "Writs of Achievement" we presented to students at the end of each semester. I signed it and framed it up as a formal presentation to him. Completely private, personal and unofficial, it was. But I'll share it with you:

Harlaxton College
The British Campus of The University of Evansville

Omnibus et Singulis
To All and To Each, to whom these Presents Shall Come,
Greetings.
Be it Known that

Dr. Zyggy Dekanski

**Having Dedicated Substantial Gifts of Knowledge, Wisdom, Care,
and Polish-Cockney Advice
To Harlaxton College and Her Students,
Is Hereby Awarded Recognition as**

Teacher of the Year

In His Special Minibus Classroom.

**Done at Harlaxton Manor, Harlaxton, England,
on the 24th day of June
in the Year of Our Lord Two Thousand Fourteen**

Signed: David Cameron, Prime Minister of Something, Somewhere
Signed: J. Gordon Kingsley, ThD, LittD, LLD, HumD, Principal of Harlaxton
College (Gone Missing)

Zyggy seemed both amused and pleased. I, of course, meant it. In irony and humor and fun, so often there is truth.

But Zyggy had the last word. Just as I was leaving Harlaxton forever and ever, Zyggy came with a plaque, which reads, "Many People Walk Through Our Lives, but Only True Friends Leave Footprints on Our Hearts." And then, almost nonchalantly, as a cover for the emotions welling up in both of us, Zyggy said, "There will be a place for this on your wall in your new home in America. There will be a place!"

And there is indeed a place, for sure there is a place, right next to my desk, where I see it every day.

Thank you, Professor Zyggy.

Your footprint is on my heart.

"Oh, You Mean *That* Boston Marathon"

We ran the Boston Marathon, did Suzanne and I.

I finished 141st. She finished before me, and came back on the course to find me.

This was not, I'm sorry to say, the Boston Marathon in Massachusetts, in which case we would have qualified ever after as bona fide world-class jocks. Instead, our marathon was in that original Boston, in England's County of Lincolnshire, 34.7 miles from Harlaxton Manor.

And so I'm also sorry to report that though I truly did finish 141st in the Boston Marathon, there were only 143 running in this one, and not the 35,671 entrants in Massachusetts last year.

Nevertheless, we can say with utter and complete honesty that we ran the Boston Marathon, and finished it!

Harlaxton sports are sometimes like that. First, and unlike most overseas study programs, Harlaxton *has* sports teams. We called them, during our years in residence, "the soon-to-be world famous Harlaxton Lions." And Harlaxton has a full-sized gym, or "sports hall" as the Brits say, with very good fitness equipment as well as free weights. To say nothing of pleasant jogging routes on the picture-book country lanes around the Manor or along the towpath of a 1700s canal.

The Harlaxton Lions regularly beat the British "air force academy," RAF Cranwell, in basketball. Used to beat everybody in basketball, but British teams got better, especially with some very big Latvian centers showing up to play. And the Lions play very competitively in volleyball—though our regular competition with a women's prison team doesn't include a home game at Harlaxton.

In 2007, the Lions basketball team went undefeated until the final game of the season, whereupon I told them we were challenging that year's NCAA Final Four Champion, the Florida Gators, to come to Harlaxton Manor and have a showdown with us in our Sports Hall, "seating capacity 3, standing room 67." Would you believe it? The Florida Gators didn't show up. Afraid, I guess. What else could we do: we straightway declared a forfeit and the next day declared ourselves the "Transatlantic Roundball Champions of the English Speaking World."

In celebration, our team members had Championship T-shirts done up—very classy on the front side, featuring our Harlaxton logo, which is based on the handsome shield-crest of Gregory Gregory himself. I was so proud of them, at least until they turned to walk away and revealed the reverse side of their quirky shirts. The backside words, in bold red? "A drinking team with a basketball problem."

Oh, well. Our Boston Marathon success was also a bit quirky. And when I told the marathon tale to a group of UK friends, one of them asked, in true British fashion and with typical British deadpan humor ("humour"),

"Oh? You say there is also a Boston in the Colonies?"

I would write occasional reports to the University of Evansville community through their weekly newsletter called AceNotes. This was a report for September 7, 2011, adapted slightly for these sketches.

"Who's That You Said You Saw in the Great Hall of Harlaxton Manor? Did You Say Kevin Spacey?"

Last Monday night [said my report to the folks back home], scenes from *Romeo and Juliet* were played in the Great Hall of Harlaxton Manor, in space similar to the great halls of Middle Temple in London and Hampton Court Palace, where Shakespeare himself once acted in his own plays.

Two former Harlaxton (Fall 1995) students were featured: Liz Morton as Juliet, Nathan Darrow as Prologue and Director. They were joined by three actors from the Old Vic Company [London's most historic and one of its best professional theatres], including world-class actor and artistic director Kevin Spacey, who played the bit part of Friar Laurence. The troupe came to Harlaxton because Nathan (a native of Kansas City, a graduate of the Theatre Department at the University of Evansville) asked them to come.

The Old Vic company are presently [I then wrote] closing a London run of Shakespeare's *Richard III*, in which Kevin Spacey is starring and Nathan Darrow has two very substantial roles (including that of Henry Richmond, the future King Henry V). The company begins a world tour of *Richard III* next week in Hong Kong.

Nathan and Liz both say that Harlaxton was a major part in their own life journeys, and they wanted to come back "home" and do something good for present students.

They did!

The scenes from *Romeo and Juliet* were outstanding. And then these two young Harlaxton grads joined Kevin Spacey, one of the greatest actors living today, as he and members of the cast answered questions from Harlaxton students. (I think every student was present, even though we had not been allowed to advertise or announce in advance, which would have created a media circus. The silent communication system of Harlaxton College is better than African drums!) Spacey quietly urged our students to follow their dreams, work hard, and "never never never" let obstacles keep them from their goals. It was a great evening.

You may wonder — though probably not — what the Principal's job is on an evening like this. It was to drive to an Italian restaurant in Grantham Town (the restaurant located, by the way, in the very place where Isaac Newton worked in an apothecary's shop — a drug store — when he was attending the King's School in Grantham) to get "pizzas and stuff" for these hungry actors to eat. I was honored to do it!

All in all, it was a very good Monday night at Harlaxton College, *where all the faculty are brilliant, all the students are above average, and the energy never stops.*

Dry Campus, Wet Pub

At Harlaxton, we managed to plant ourselves quite firmly on all sides of the alcohol "issue."

And, remarkably, students accepted our official (I hope not officious) hypocrisy, or at the very best our ambiguity, taking it all in stride. Maybe it was an important part of their education for adulthood, where most things are not black-and-white clear. Or maybe I'm just rationalizing.

Jut look at what always felt to me like "the mess" and which always had for me the feel of some medieval theologians sitting around and splitting theological hairs, an activity famously critiqued by the twelfth-century French scholar Pierre Abélard in his *Sic et Non* ("Yes and No"):

Sic. Students were, the minute they touched down in Britain, legal to drink — whatever the laws had been back in their home state.

Non. But Harlaxton, following the home University of Evansville, was a "dry" campus. No booze in rooms.

Sic. But we served wine at "nice" College dinners, following the practices of "civilized" European society.

Sic. And we actually operated a College pub, "The Bistro," where we didn't serve the hard stuff, but offered enough beer and wine and such-like that students could, and on occasion some did, get pretty drunk.

Non. But if students were drunk and disorderly, from drinking in the Grantham clubs or drinking in our in-house pub or drinking alcohol "smuggled" into their rooms — the smuggling really wasn't that hard, for there were never any consistent checks on what came into the Manor — then the students were disciplined, usually with fines and sometimes with both fines and "community service."

So, our official virtue was at the very least tarnished, and I'm afraid we wore our administrative purity with a quite rakish and confused air.

(For me, I guess, administering this confusing kind of policy had begun several years earlier, when we would regularly do a morning pick-up of the beer cans that were trashing the very fine and very beautiful Baptist-related campus I served as President. And I would tell the Baptist preachers with solemn-sober humor—which they readily understood, from knowing their own children and those in their pews—that "those Rockhurst boys" from the nearby Jesuit college "had been on our campus again, throwing their cans around." I guess we all understood, at some level, that most Baptists were only human and that the "real Baptist rule" on alcohol, as a Baptist friend and colleague would occasionally tell me, reads like this: "Baptists *never* drink—*long pause here, then quietly*— in front of each other.")

Our "real rule" at Harlaxton, in fact, was that people either should not drink or should drink responsibly, in either case not becoming a problem to others in our very small, very serious educational community. Drunks can create a problem, as can self-righteous carpers.

But why did we do this, I keep wondering? Why did we carry forward an official public "morality" that often ran counter to the real lives of men and women everyday and everywhere? Why didn't we just say to these adults, "It's your choice and your responsibility, for both actions and consequences"?

Darned if I know, but it is the way the world works. And in most cases, it is probably better to hold to high standards and then offer, and receive, support and discipline and forgiveness when we fail. Maybe, in fact, it is not hypocrisy at all, but a necessary ambiguity of life for those of us described by the American poet e e cummings as "humans merely being," people living in a world of imperfect mortals, including ourselves.

I'll drink to that. Moderately.

"Free Coffee In The Bistro!"

A short time after some of our really, really good Maintenance Staff folks had completely refurbished the Bistro so that it was not only functional again but even spiffy, our students began hinting—aw, heck, there was no hinting about it: they were just saying it out loud and clear—what a good idea it would be to use this place as a Coffee House in the afternoon in addition to having it as an in-house Pub at night.

Sounded good to me. Our kids could study down there, have meetings with profs or other students, enjoy chatting with each other, watch the big-screen television we had bought at Curry's and installed as part of the deal. Probably some students would use it as a Coffee House who wouldn't use it as a Pub, and vice versa—seemed a good idea to make the place attractive and useful to as many students as we could.

So we invested in some pretty fancy and high-powered coffee equipment, like at Starbucks or Costa, then hired a person to staff it in the afternoons, then opened up for business, with prices for coffee about a pound cheaper per cup than at the coffee shop chains. And, we bought some really nice, really big coffee cups, which I loved. Big white cups with a big bold black "**Harlaxton College**" on their sides. Wish I had one.

We had got ourselves equipped, were ready, were organized, could run with the big coffee dogs and provide a great place and a great service to our students.

So we announced, promoted, and had a Grand Opening for our new Bistro Coffee Shop, "opened by public demand."

And nothing happened. Nobody came to the party.

Now, disappointed if not crushed, we tried to figure out what was wrong. Nice place. Good coffee and hot chocolate and other stuff. Good price. The students had said they wanted this. It all added up to a plus for everybody. Except, nobody came.

So we did some "market research" — not hard to do at Harlaxton, where you just ask folks in the Refectory or as you see them around the Manor what's going on. The "market research" went something like this:

"How come people aren't using the coffee shop in the Bistro?"

"Prices are too high."

"But Harlaxton prices are lower than anywhere else, and we've got to meet our costs. We're just trying to provide a service, not make a profit."

"Still too high."

"But you buy the coffee at your home campus."

"Yes, but it's different here."

"How is it different here?"

"I don't know — it's just — different."

Well, that information helped a lot! "I don't know — it's just — different." So much for market research. It just didn't seem very rational at all, but we did hear one part of the message loud and clear.

And we cut the price of the coffee.

Still no takers. Cut prices again. Still nobody. Cut again, now down to £1 a cup. A few wandered in and drank the coffee, but nowhere near enough to pay for the coffee itself and the salary of a staff person, to say nothing of the cost of the machines. Now the mystery deepens.

"Shall we cut the price again?" we sage and wise administrators asked ourselves. And we tried fifty pence. Helped a bit with business, but just a bit. This is 50p I'm talkin' about, for a big cup of coffee good as at Starbucks!

"Okay, okay," someone said in one of our Administrative Cabinet meetings, "what if we just give it away?" (You wonder what those important administrators do in those important staff meetings? They talk about the price of coffee in the Bistro!)

So we tried that. It worked good. People came, drank the coffee, studied, chatted — all just like it was planned in the first place.

Except they ripped off all the very nice **Harlaxton College** coffee cups — "souvenirs," you know, stuffed into a lot of bags that went back to America, I'm sure.

We couldn't justify keeping a paid staff person to serve free coffee, but the answer to that dilemma was a bonus for all: spouses of our Visiting Faculty from America, indeed some of the faculty members themselves, began volunteering (well, we asked them to volunteer and pushed it pretty hard). They took the necessary training and began serving as baristas. They liked doing it, they liked the "I Major in Coffee" T-shirts that we had made up for them, they liked the time with their colleague-friends and with their students in this informal setting. And students enjoyed seeing their faculty and families as "real people," and as servants.

(As a side note, I should add that one of the very good things about Harlaxton was its human, down to earth, "let's do what we can do attitude" on the part of our faculty and just about everyone else. I'm telling you the truth: profs who would gritch and sulk and complain at their home university would often just pitch in, volunteer, and help out at Harlaxton — just like it used to be in colleges before they became so stratified and compartmentalized and sometimes nasty.)

So, in the end of all, this student idea was a genuine success. Our students came, drank their free coffee, studied etc., were served by their faculty baristas, kept their "souvenir" coffee cups well hidden and are no doubt enjoying them today back home in America.

We lost money on it, of course, from beginning to end. But, hey, some things are more important than money. Isn't that one of the big lessons a good college teaches?

Bob, The Swan

Few colleges can boast a pet swan.

Harlaxton College did.

A pet swan named Bob.

It began with one of our former Gardeners, I think, who brought the swan to Harlaxton as a rescue project from one of Britain's many agencies that care for animals: the Royal Society for the Protection of Birds, maybe; or perhaps the Swan Sanctuary—I think it was that; or possibly the Royal Society for the Prevention of Cruelty to Animals.

In any case, this lovely animal arrived with a totally and irreparably shattered wing.

Pat, the Gardener, named him "Bob." She looked after him, even coming from her home on weekends and holidays to feed him, even making sure he had his annual two-week holiday back at the shelter with other swans. That's right: a two-week vacation. Maybe all swans in Britain don't take vacations, but ours did.

Once at Harlaxton, Bob settled into his nice home on the reflecting pool—called the "Dutch Canal"—in the Manor's lovely side gardens.

Then one summer, while on his holiday back at the shelter for swans, Bob apparently had a "summer romance," and so Pat came back with two swans.

Like a lot of Harlaxton couples do, Bob and new friend got along well for a while, swimming placidly on the reflecting pool, so that now Harlaxton's beautiful swan-picture was doubled. But then, sadly and mysteriously, all swan-hell broke loose. Bob became angry, grumpy, irascible, nasty. He kept trying to kill the new swan. So what could be done: Pat took the new arrival back to the sanctuary.

I don't know if other swans came and went — Pat would know and could tell us. But mostly Bob just became a grumpy old guy, didn't want other swans around, nor did they want to be around. Swans are notoriously ill tempered, anyway; and in one of those amusing and eccentric facts of British history, they can be as ornery as they wish because it is the King himself or the Queen herself who has owned all the unmarked swans in Britain since 1198 (and probably before). Why would that be so? Because in earlier eras swans were something of a table-meat delicacy.

So maybe Bob just got uppity, with a royal owner and all that.

Harlaxton students of course "adopted" Bob, "borrowed" bread from the Refectory to feed him, tried to treat him nice and be treated nice in return. It worked in one direction. Our students were nice; Bob was still grumpy, sometimes scary and hissy and threatening.

Then, one glorious day, Pat announced that a swan had been found who would mate with Bob, and more amazing, with whom Bob would mate. Her name was "Viv." Together, like they were posing for a post card, Bob and Viv would float at their peaceful, picturesque ease, icons of Harlaxton calm. Many were the photos snapped of two graceful white swans floating on their deep blue pool, with the golden stones of Harlaxton Manor reflected on the waters.

Things and swans floated along just fine, in fact, until breeding season, when Bob and Viv began fighting fiercely and would not stop. A clever Biology professor from our faculty decided to check — he says it is not easy to do or to tell — and came up with the explanation, which had the force of revelation. Viv was a boy!

So off to the big lake under the stone bridge on the front lane went Viv, where to my knowledge HE lives to this day.

Bob stayed on his reflecting pool, still grumpy, still fed by students, still showing little appreciation. Then Bob seemed to get swan-Alzheimer's and began wandering, stumbling an awkward path all the way from the side garden, across or around the front circle of Schroeder Courtyard, around the Great Courtyard Gates and Wall, up the little hill into Pegasus Courtyard. It must have taken him hours, for swans swim or fly — they don't hike. And there Bob would hold court, the Grumpy Swan King of Pegasus Court, being fed more bread purloined from the Refectory than ever he could have imagined. Maybe he was not demented after all, just clever.

Alas, it all came to an end, for Bob died — of natural causes. He was found "at home," lifelessly floating on his reflecting pool, as if his spirit were now free to move in and out of the mystical doors and windows of the blessed Harlaxton home mirrored on his own waters. It happened on a Saturday, and such is our technology-rich world that by that evening word of his passing had gone out around the globe, with Harlaxton students and alumni writing in with their laments from countries and continents at the four points of the compass.

Pat having moved on, a new team of Harlaxton Gardeners had the grim task of burying Bob — in an unmarked grave. Such is the fate of grumpy old swans.

Yet who can doubt that he lives on in many Harlaxton memories, where he floats with un-grumpy grace on the eternally smooth surface of an eternally beautiful reflecting pool set against the eternally golden stone of beautiful Harlaxton Manor. Maybe it is as close to heaven as a grumpy old swan can get — even though he was once owned by the Queen.

R.I.P. BOB.

The White Trash Party

And so, student Chris Landers came to the door of the Principal's Lodge, rang the tinny doorbell, and gave us a *personal invitation* to the White Trash Party.

"The what?"

"The White Trash Party. In the Bistro. Tonight. Sponsored by the Student Government Association — sort of."

Well, I knew the engaging Chris Landers well enough to know that the party was probably sponsored mostly by Chris and some of his friends. And I knew it would be interesting and lively.

"Here. I've made a poster. Mind if I tape one to your door?"

And so, for the first and only time in our near-dozen years at Harlaxton, an advert for a White Trash Party in our College pub was posted on the very principal-y front door of the College's very official Principal's Lodge.

And that poster, I tell you, was a bona fide piece of folk art: at the top, a grand picture of an American flag; then, in big letters, "White Trash Party"; and below that, a picture of an old guy with a cigarette butt dangling from his lower lip. The old guy was wearing a baseball cap and big ugly boots and bib overalls (Big Smith) and a flannel shirt with left sleeve rolled up to stash a pack of cigarettes, and he was standing by a battered pickup truck. And then the legend underneath the picture: "You May Not Be One But Somebody in Your Family Surely Is. God Bless America." And date and time and place.

Oh, jeepers: it was a work night, and I was laboring hard at the computer trying to meet a deadline, and we were weary to the bone, and anyway I never felt the Principal and Spouse were particular assets at a student party.

But Chris had invited us personally!

We talked back and forth about it until nearly 9:00pm, then decided if we were going we had to go right then, and decided "yes." Suzanne went back to the bedroom and in ten minutes came out scary: this very attractive woman had somehow frizzed her striking red hair into a something approaching a bitch-do; and I don't even know where she found the trashy clothes she threw on or how she made her chest stand out in such a dramatic protrusion. As for me, I was also in just moments the old poster-guy himself, without the pickup truck—what crummy clothes we keep in our closets long past their useful lives!

And so we showed up at the party for thirty minutes or so, until Suzanne whispered "I can't keep holding my back like this." And, as I thought would be the case, we were largely ignored by the students who were having their own fun and joining God in blessing America.

I am glad we went. It seemed like a great party, and Chris was pleased. I left the poster up for a few days, 'cause I really liked it. Wish I'd kept it.

Maybe I did—who knows what's in the boxes in the upstairs closet, as yet unpacked!

God Bless America!

Naked Mile Lane

That's not its real name, of course.

I don't even know if it has a real name, that mile of narrow lane leading up to Harlaxton Manor from the A607 highway, through the Great Front Gates, between two farm fields, over the stone-banistered bridge, past the soccer field, through the Gatehouse, and through the gates of Schroeder Courtyard up to the Manor doors itself. (I know, I know, as our Engineering students made mathematically clear, the lane is only .78 or .91 of a mile long, depending on where you start and end. But, hey, we are talking here Poetry, not Engineering.)

And, name or not, the lane has a history. And legends. Oh, such legends. They tell me, even, that people ran that lane, well, *naked*.

I don't actually know anything at all about the Naked Mile, of course. Never did. Principals don't know such things. But I do know that when I was a faculty member at Harlaxton in 1976 it didn't exist, but by 2003, when I returned as Principal, it was an established institution.

I would hear rumors, of course. Things like these:

That students would run naked in packs, as well as alone;

That in some semesters the question was not "Have you run The Mile?" but rather "How many times have you run The Mile?"

That in some semesters there was even a Century Club of those who had run The Mile 100 times or more;

That taxis would come filled with "Townies" who wanted to watch, the drivers making sure to keep their bright lights fixed on the lane in hopes of seeing something interesting (that one sounds a little far-fetched to me, but maybe it is true).

And I had a few actual, first-hand experiences of this thing I didn't and don't know about. Things such as

A slender girl, now a respected nurse, leaping into a shallow ditch to avoid headlights, only to find that the ditch was filled with brambles. She came to class the next day totally scratched up and gouged with dramatic though shallow cuts. And that was on the flesh that we could see;

A visiting administrator and wife from a respected university, the dad keeping lookout and the mom videotaping as their high-school age sons ran The Mile;

Two male students rushing naked through the front door of the Manor just as the parents of a young and new professor were checking in for a visit—both parents being medical doctors from Germany. The professor's mother spoke rapidly to her son, in German and with considerable animation, and I later asked him what she had said. Dr. Rudolph Glitz, now a much-respected professor at the University of Amsterdam, smiled his sly grin: "She said, 'Nice view.'"

A handsome faculty wife covering her chest with her hands and arms when she unexpectedly came upon students while running The Mile, only to be advised later that the proper response would have been to cover her face.

When I arrived at Harlaxton as Principal, our "General Store," later renamed "The Boutique" (still sounds a little posh to me for the range of goods we offered), was selling Naked Mile T-shirts with stick figures saying, "I ran the mile bare-bottomed style." The home campus expressed some concern about this, and so I retrieved the shirts and stuffed them into a cabinet in the Principal's Office. And what then appeared as replacements? Classy T-shirts saying "Harlaxton Track. The 0.9 Mile Run." (No one could have possibly divined their hidden meaning!)

Occasionally, when taking my frequent jogs by daylight (clothed), I would pick up intimate garments on the lane. I took to tacking these up on the notice board by Schroeder Lounge along with an ever-so-formal sign that read something like, "The Principal descried [sic] this garment while jogging on the footpath and hereby returns it to its rightful owner." But no one ever said "Thanks."

And my one "visual" of this thing I knew nothing about was on a Halloween night, when we were returning to campus in a taxi. Three girls were standing by the Walled Garden stark naked except for witches' hats perched quite adroitly on their lovely heads. I told the driver to go straight on by and to see nothing at all. But he didn't. Instead he stopped, rolled down the window, and called out in a lusty voice,

"Trick or Treat!"

"Going Out" to the Clubs

There's no point in my even trying to write about "The Clubs" and the lure they had for some — a good minority — of our students.

I know I am old, but it just made no sense to me. It never made sense to me when I was young, either.

Why would our girls dress up in those tiny little semi-dresses and shiver their way into Grantham town on a freezing night to drink at The Goose or Gravity and meet some guys they would never want to take home to mother. What's the point? To live dangerously? Close to the edge?

Maybe there was nothing else for them to do at that time of night. But the same kids did the same things in London, where there was plenty to do.

My predecessor as Principal used to tell the students not to go to certain clubs in town, naming them by name. He behaved more responsibly than I did, I guess, though I once quizzically suggested he was just giving them a shopping list if they were inclined to frequent these kinds of spots.

So I watched them go, night-by-night, semester-by-semester, hoping they would get back home to Harlaxton safely.

You can tell I still can't figure it out. Probably won't.

Jan Beckett, our Vice Principal for Academic Affairs, College Librarian, and Magistrate in the English Court system not only described it best but also gave the best possible caution when she suggested to some students that going to some of these places might be "feeding off the bottom of the gene pool."

But I think they kept nibbling.

"The P's Are Coming!"

It wasn't a student who said it, but one of our faculty members. An engaging young Theatre prof from William Jewell College named Nathan Wyman.

"The P's are coming!"

"The P's are coming?" I asked. "Who or what are the P's?"

"Parents. My parents are coming to visit."

And they did.

It's good that they did. It's good when they do. And they do a lot. Parents do come to Harlaxton a lot.

There are seasons when they come in larger numbers— Thanksgiving, mid-semesters, even Easter when it is early. But they come 'most any time of any semester, so *happy* to see their son or daughter, who is in turn so *happy* to see them.

You would watch them in the Refectory, at first fumbling around to know where the dishes and silverware were, then smiling to hear it called "crockery and cutlery" by our British staff, then figuring out how to work the darn coffee machine, which of course has a mind of its own as coffee machines do in whatever country they exist, then looking like they might feel a bit out of place, a bit uncomfortable, among all those lively students. Soon, though, a little family scene would form at a table, as if everyone else had just disappeared, even in that large and handsome and crowded Refectory, and Mom and Dad and son or daughter were alone together as if sitting at their own kitchen table. Nice.

I would usually approach the P's, usually in the Refectory—learn who they were, where they were from, tell them how good their son or daughter was as part of the Harlaxton community (I told the truth, and usually that was the truth), ask if we could help in any way, ask what they were doing while they were visiting.

And here's where the most remarkable thing became apparent. Roles were reversed. Now it was the son or the daughter acting as parent, calling the shots, planning the schedules, deciding where they would go and when. It was the son or daughter explaining to the P's that it really might *not* be possible to get to Scotland, Ireland, and London on the same afternoon. (Americans must be the most ambitious travelers in the world!) It was the son or daughter saying, "You must see this," "We should eat there," "This is a great experience." They sometimes even adopted British ways of saying it, like "This is not to be missed."

What we were looking at was the future. The future, when son or daughter would be grown and in the prime of life, taking more leadership in the family, is it too much to say "taking responsibility for" the P's, their parents. It was a little glimpse into tomorrow, right there in the Harlaxton Refectory.

Oh, occasionally a particularly threatened or blustery dad would make it a point to regain control, by sheer force of habit and male dominance. But more often the parents would begin to smile, first in a happy surprise that "my girl" or "my boy" was taking such initiative "for me," then in a recognition that he or she really does know more than I do about this place and how to spend these days, and finally in a sense of relief that someone who really knows something is in charge and, even more, that she really is growing up into a woman, he really *is* becoming a man.

It was nice to see, and I know from experience as a father that it is nice to feel.

So we were always glad to see the P's. We had nice guest rooms in the Manor, mostly for when the P's could come. And it was always good, on behalf of son or daughter, to welcome the P's into the *Harlaxton* Family.

I never knew what it was like when our students went back home. Everyone probably slipped back into the old routines, the comfortable roles. It is hard to change our habits of life, and a familiar place usually leads us back to familiar ways of acting.

But having seen what a son or daughter could do, the P's must have had a new respect, a new confidence, a new sense of anticipation and hope, even joy, at what "my girl," or "my boy," might become in life.

How could they not?

The P's had seen the Preview at Harlaxton.

The Look of Wow!

"Wow!"

Of such the eloquence of student Tyler Tines, catching his first glimpse of Harlaxton Manor from the top of the lane—eloquence reflected in one of our very best Harlaxton videos. There's Tyler: yellow T-shirt, jeans, cap turned backwards, eyes looking at a beauty and majesty such as he has never seen before, mind taking in the fact that Harlaxton Manor is about to be his home, and the camera catches his "Wow!"

And The Look.

I remember it so well, for in that single word and that instinctive gaze were a thousand volumes, a million pictures, of how students and alums see Harlaxton.

We even called it "The Look." "The Look of 'Wow'"!

Over and over again it happened.

New students, ragged after a day and night on airplanes, hauling big bags through airports, enduring three hours on a bus from Heathrow to Harlaxton, arriving bone-weary and eye-bedraggled and soul-pitiful, and yet, and yet, as we stood at the Great Oak Door to greet them one by one off the buses ("Welcome to Harlaxton." "Welcome Home"), there it was, every time. The Look. A sense of wonder, a sense of amazement, a sense of hope, a sense of promise, a sense of—well, a sense of "Wow!" There, in their weary eyes, The Look. There, in their weary voices, The "Wow!"

And alumni, sometimes bringing a husband or wife, or even children, to see the place they had loved so much. Finally they had come back, in their hearts had come "home" again. And though no spouse or child could ever understand it however much they loved, however much they tried, across the eyes of their Harlaxton alum came The Look — eyes a bit misty, looking far into the past, deep into the heart of memory, far into the future. And then, then, then, came the quiet words, spoken almost in a whisper, as if in a soft prayer of thanksgiving: "Harlaxton changed my life." The "Wow" of Experience.

The fact is, Harlaxton did change our lives, does change lives. Student, faculty, faculty child, electrician, security person, principal—all of us found, find, that "Blessed Harlaxton, My Home" changes our lives forever, and for good.

What can we do, then, but gaze in gratitude into our deepest heart of life and love and experience? The Look.

And what else can we say?

Just, "Wow"

The Harlaxton Family Thanksgiving

I am writing this little essay during Thanksgiving week, in the fifth month after leaving the rich life of Harlaxton College. And this Thursday, this Thanksgiving Day, will be much, much different from the last eleven.

We will gather together what family can come — our kids are in Chicago, Atlanta, and Fukuoka, Japan, and they all live busy lives, and so it is a gift that the Chicago contingent can and will make the effort to join us on Turtle Creek in good ole Beloit, Wisconsin, USA.

Suzanne will cook a sumptuous meal, a blend of culinary delight and artistic pleasure — something she loves to do and has not been able to do for some years. We will give thanks for the graces of God, the many undeserved but most welcome gifts of God. We will enjoy the festive meal, we will enjoy one another, we may take a glance or two (or more) at some American football on the telly, and we will relish the peaceful scenes of Americana outside the large glass windows that form much of the back wall of our native stone house:

> The stands of native woodlands, including great ancient oaks, and the broad and shallow rushing river that is Turtle Creek;

> Maybe some deer gracefully tracking through a layer of soft snows;

> Certainly some waterfowl dropping in for a squawking visit, on their way south for the winter;

> And small animals like the squirrels and chipmunks and too-tame raccoons busily collecting last bits of acorns and nuts and other provender before winter weather gets even more severe.

> We can hope that Hobart, the friendly white goose from down the creek, will pay a call, though he hasn't been around since the snows began arriving — or maybe we just can't see him in the snow.

I'm not sure, but I think the numerous wild turkeys may be lying low this week—Thanksgiving in America is not particularly friendly to turkeys.

This current blanket of snow cover, our second snow already for this year, is beautiful, truly beautiful, almost beautiful enough to make us forget the sub-freezing 20° Fahrenheit/-7° Celsius just outside the windows.

The grandbabies, now "big girls" of almost-three and almost-five—as I am learning, children look ahead *anticipating*, grandparents look back *remembering*—make it all very special by their sense of wonder at it all. I have long thought that God gives us a second chance, as our children are growing up, to see the world through fresh eyes, those eyes of wonder. And now, with grandchildren, the astounding gift of a third chance!

One could do worse than spend a quiet Thanksgiving Day on Turtle Creek.

What we will miss, of course, is the larger community that is Harlaxton College, as it gathers for the deep down good celebration of a Harlaxton Family Thanksgiving.

The Thanksgiving Service in the Great Hall was always rich and meaningful to me, as our students reached across oceans and miles to say "Thank You" to, and with, moms and dads and brothers and sisters and families.

"I am so grateful for being at Harlaxton and for all I have gained here, all that has been done for me and with me in this place, among these people."

"I am thankful for my parents, my family and friends in America, for all who have made Harlaxton possible."

"I thank God for his love."

And God's loving presence was clearly felt among those of us living in Harlaxton, as well as by visiting friends and families.

The hymns and songs, the readings from the Holy Bible, the prayers—all "fit" the place and the occasion, bringing back echoes of the years when the Great Hall was a chapel for the resident Jesuit priests and the people in communities around the Manor.

And then, after the Thanksgiving Service, we moved to the State Dining Room for the buffet, the Harlaxton Thanksgiving Dinner: "Happy Thanksgiving." "Happy Thanksgiving to you, as well."

We were first greeted by the big turkey that Catering Manager Tony Sheridan had on display at the beginning of the buffet line—students always joked that he froze it and brought it out again next year, the "Eternal Turkey." And we sat down for the feast in the Long Gallery, with plenty of seconds.

No student or American faculty member could ever know the hours spent by Suzanne and Tony Sheridan and our Catering Staff to get the meal just right for Americans, from the menu selection to seasoning the meal just like it would have been at home—different from British seasonings. I remember when a student told her mother on Skype that the meal was indeed "just like home," and her mother said, "You're not just saying that to make me feel good, are you?" and her daughter said, "No, it as much like home as it could be without you and Dad," and they both started to cry. "Happy Thanksgiving."

Many times, if the weather were right, we would have a fire in the giant hearth of the Great Hall, and sometimes a Dr. Baker or a Dr. Magennis or a Dr. Bujak or a Dr. Green or even a whole group of British and American faculty would hold forth, with spirited conversations and/or rank foolishness that could go on into the night.

In fact, the great building herself, Harlaxton Manor, seemed to relax, to let her great and awesome architectural power express itself in a kindly warmth, a domestic gentleness, that always felt like a welcoming "home." We were all thankful for Harlaxton Manor, but it felt on this day—as we prayed and feasted and shared a joy with one another--that she was glad, too, for us. People and Place become somehow one.

All in all, the Harlaxton Family Thanksgiving was one of the most beautiful experiences, and in one of the most beautiful settings, any of us had ever known.

So, yes, this Thanksgiving will be good on Turtle Creek. No complaints. No laments.

But we will still miss Harlaxton Manor, and the Harlaxton Family Thanksgiving, and that larger Harlaxton family that was, every year, every semester, joined together by a grand purpose to know our world better and make it a better place, to know ourselves better and become a better people, and to drink in the Thanksgiving Day gifts of living in an astonishingly beautiful place with some down-home good and gifted people.

It was Community.

It was Family.

It was Harlaxton.

It was Home.

The Harlaxton Family Christmas

We never even caught our breath between the Harlaxton Family Thanksgiving and the Harlaxton Family Christmas.

Thursday: Thanksgiving.

Friday: Christmas Begins.

We had to do it that way, because students would be leaving for home or end-of-semester travels in just a couple of weeks. At Harlaxton, Christmas had to come early.

So, on Friday, up would go the giant Christmas Tree in the Great Hall. I always said it was twenty-five feet tall—it looked like it to me. Suzanne, who knew better because she helped put it up, said it was closer to twelve feet. But it surely filled up a whole lot of the space on the Great Hall stage, and its top reached the highest edge of the rich wood paneling—telling the huge Atlantide figures, forever in anguish along the wall, to move over a bit, to make way for Christmas. That Christmas tree, I tell you, was beautiful, whatever its shape, whatever the year.

Our Gardeners and House Team and Maintenance Team worked hard first thing in the morning to get the giant thing through the doors and into the hall. The Gardeners and Suzanne would decorate and light the highest part of the tree before it was with great effort hoisted up and embedded in its huge box—also made by our staff folks. It was never easy.

But our staff unfailingly delivered, for by 2:00 or 2:30, when students came in for the "tree-trimming," the Great Tree was always standing proudly in place, Lord of Christmas for that year.

At the tree trimming, we all turned into kids. Hot chocolate, brownies, popcorn, Christmas carols. Ornaments and icicles on a table, waiting to be attached to the tree. (Have you any idea how hard it is to buy icicles in England? Couldn't do it—brought them in from America.) Students and faculty and staff members joining in the decorating, the "tree-trimming." Lots of photographs. Lots of talk. Nice to hear the Christmas music. Nice to see the tree taking shape. Nice snacks. It's beginning to feel a lot like Christmas.

Well, sir, we had only a week for it to "feel like" Christmas before it actually happened: the Harlaxton Family Christmas. And it was a huge event. On a Saturday. First day of final exams.

By now the whole of Harlaxton Manor was decorated, and what a magnificent Christmas house it becomes. The Catering Staff had been preparing a Christmas Buffet bounty for days — a spread never to be forgotten. The House Team had the place set up perfectly.

Afternoon was for staff, and it was beautiful. Each staff member was invited to bring any and all family members, and we would see our workers all dressed up in festive clothes, especially handsome and attractive as "real people" and not in their accustomed uniforms or work-wear. We would meet their partners and spouses, their precious and wide-eyed children, and we would know them in a different way, a more complete way. Often, our seasoned workers would bring both children and grandchildren. Persons whom we knew only as the ones who did the heavy lifting or the careful craftsmanship would now appear to us as loving parents and grandparents, helping a little one make a Christmas card for his "mummy," or an angel for the Christmas tree.

I tell you, it was beautiful. It was beautiful. Every year it was beautiful.

There were Christmas crackers, of course. A wonderful invention that deserves mass acceptance in the American Colonies. And music. And Christmas crafts for the children, often led by Ellen Welsh with Nursing students or Education students or members of our Christian Fellowship working one to one with the kiddies. And Father Christmas, Zyggy Dekanski most years doing the honors as the perfect Santa. And a gift for every child.

It was Christmas. It was really Christmas.

Then, after this session, a few of us would scurry around to do a quick cleanup, and we would do it all over again in the evening and night—this time the Harlaxton Family Christmas for our students and faculty and Meet-a-Family hosts.

At this event, members of the Harlaxton Collegiate Choir would sing carols as the guests arrived in the Entry Hall, through the Great Oak Door. The buffet feast, again. Caroling in the Great Hall. And then, for those who wished it, a trek through Harlaxton Village— often a very cold trek through Harlaxton Village, giant flashlights ("torches") in hand—to sing carols for homebound persons. It is hard to find a place in America, any more, where it is safe to go Christmas caroling, or where people welcome it. But in Harlaxton Village, we could relive the history and the traditions of Christmas without fret. Kevin Lawry of the Harlaxton Village Church would most often prearrange the houses for us to visit and lead us on the tour, and each year we finished at the home of George and Christine Beasley, right next to the church.

George and Christine Beasley. On their own, without prompting or pleading (and in fact, each year I would tell them they didn't need to go to all this trouble for us), Christine and some helpers would bake delicious pastries from her native Germany, and George would prepare delicious hot mulled wine which he would serve to us out of the "boot" of his car; and as we were singing to them "We Wish You a Merry Christmas," they were plying us with the makings of a *very* merry Christmas. One year, George and Christine even gave us the most beautiful Christmas Tree we ever had for the Harlaxton Family Christmas, a giant sentinel that took pride of place as "our Harlaxton Christmas Tree" in the Great Hall. It came right out of their own front yard ("garden"). "It was blocking the light," they explained.

So many good people, doing so many good things! Christmas!

Then we would trudge home again to Harlaxton Manor, passing the mysterious strong shape of the village church in the deep midwinter darkness, making our way through that deep dark and cold, our torches showing the way, hoping that some of the after-meal hot chocolate was still left for us. One thing we could always count on, and did — a roaring fire in the six-foot high fireplace in the Great Hall.

Well, that's the scene. We have left it all behind, now, but each of us stores up memories in our lives, and those memories stand beside us in difficult days and in happy days.

I think I shall never have better memories, happier memories, warmer memories, than those of our Harlaxton Family Christmas, where the old Christmas traditions came alive again, the winter cold was warmed, and the Star of Hope rode high in the skies,

not only over Bethlehem,

but over Harlaxton as well.

Harlaxton Manor:
Miracle, Mystery, Drama

Of course, the main thing about Harlaxton Manor is—well, Harlaxton Manor.

She is just **there**, in your face, down the lane and across the fields, a miracle of gloriously golden stone when standing proud in a slant of English sun, a kind of solid-eerie gray eminence when under a hovering cloud-cover, a warmly-welcoming refuge when bathed in soft floodlights on a crisp, cool English night.

She is just **there**. Harlaxton.

One April night, after a Harlaxton "graduation" service in the village church, a group of us were walking back to the Manor rather than taking the shuttle bus. As we walked up the lane toward "our home," a beautiful round full moon hung suspended just above the Conservatory, as if it, too, were coming home to Harlaxton. The floodlights were on the face of the Manor, bathing it in a kind of soft under-lighting to the boldness of the moonlight; the dark night was still and quiet, stars etching their patterns in the blackness above; and, helplessly, happily, we felt the tears of joy well up in our eyes at the sheer, inescapable, unimaginable, unmitigated beauty of this place, this scene, this night.

Then, every year, some of us would gather at the top of the lane at the time of Summer Solstice, standing just inside the ironwork bars of the Great Front Gates, so that customers of The Greg must have wondered if we were prisoners trying to escape, and we would watch the setting sun reflect from the Manor windows as if they were blazing fires from a vast spaceship settled down in a Lincolnshire field. No other word describes it but Magnificent!

And then you go inside, where the marble and plasterwork and gilding and woodwork and fabrics of the state rooms exhibit—yes, that's the word, "exhibit"—a near-gaudy, yet still tasteful over-the-top baroque grandeur that says just what builder Gregory Gregory meant for it to say 170 years ago: This Is a Great House. This Is a *Stately* Home.

So theatrical is Harlaxton, as an architectural masterpiece, that "once upon a time," on a visit, Evansville businessman Burkley McCarthy looked all around at this Harlaxton "thing," smiled a bemused smile, and said to me, "You've got a lot of props here, Gordon." And we did.

In fact, Harlaxton is high theatre in many ways, including the things that go on inside the great house as well as the theatricality of the building itself. The British Studies course itself can be viewed as a long-running play — on-stage in the Long Gallery for twenty-five years or so, the script changing gently from time to time as new actors come into the cast. The whole curriculum and co-curriculum smacks of a lively "medieval fayre," complete with theatrical "pageant wagons," offering delights and practical necessities to excited residents and pilgrims. Inside the house there is music, there is dance, there is feasting, there is resting, there is love, there are dreams and hopes, there are lessons and sermons, there is sanctity, there is ribaldry. Harlaxton is a stage on which is played a microcosm of life. That's what theatre is. That's what theatre does.

Indeed, inside and out, Harlaxton is a miracle.

But not just any miracle. She is *our* miracle. The wonder of it all is what we felt that April night coming from the village church: this magnificent place is *our home*. And so we got to know her very well.

Which wasn't easy. We used to say it was "institutional policy" for every new student and faculty member to be lost for at least two weeks in Harlaxton Manor. And to enjoy the discoveries they made while being "lost." We posted maps by the "lift" (elevator) — I never knew why. The maps may have made sense to some people, but to me they just dramatized the total irrationality of the interior layout. A giant, 3-D, live-in jigsaw puzzle. I kept thinking that along about 2017 someone will find some student who got lost in 1989, still wandering and wondering how to find his or her lonesome and solitary way to the Library or Refectory.

We gave students free rein—or was it reign—of the house, for it truly is their home. And it was always a wonder to me how well they took care of it. Very little vandalism, and when trashing occurred it was connected to alcohol (which of course made it worse rather than excusing it). But get this: even the drunks didn't deface the beautiful State Rooms. Oh, there was that couple, drunk with love, who carved their eternal commitments in irreplaceable stone just by the lift staircase. I hope they stayed together, for making that statement cost them about seven hundred quid for repairs. But that was a rare exception.

I'm glad students took care of the house, for I always thought that Harlaxton Manor herself was our best teacher—though several of our faculty vied for and deserved that title through the years. To live in Harlaxton Manor, to walk through that house every day, to inquire into her meanings and secrets and lore, was itself a liberal education. One became truly immersed in art, in architecture, in domestic history, in social and political history, in economics, in mathematics, in engineering, in music, in drama—the list could go on and on and on. The house spoke to us, and I for one spoke back, thanking her, chatting with her, all the time.

One of her clearest lessons—and I passed it on to generations of students—is Gregory Gregory's carving his Latin inscription in huge stone letters at the front of the house, just below the clock and flagpoles: "Gregory Built These Buildings *Perfectly.*" I would often ponder that saying carved in stone: Gregory dedicated his whole life to creating Harlaxton Manor. It was his pride and joy, where he spent his money, his life's work. This huge stately home, with all those rooms, all set up for a grand family—even though he was a bachelor. And he didn't mess around or cut corners: he built a great, great, great stately home. "Gregory Built These Buildings *Perfectly.*"

He could not have, 170 years ago, even in his wildest imaginings, envisioned 150-175 students from American colleges living in his house, pursuing their studies, preparing to go out into our world to make it a better place. Couldn't have dreamed it. Yet, because he did his work well—*perfectly*—we were able to come to England, to study and work, to prepare ourselves so that we can offer to life what we are destined to offer—so that we, too, can do *our* life's work *Perfectly*. Gregory "being dead yet speaketh," teaching all of us through the ministrations of his great house. "I did my great work *perfectly*; now you go and do your work great works *perfectly*."

You notice I often say "she," and "her" when I speak of Harlaxton. For me, Harlaxton is alive, and for me she is a beautiful older lady—like the city of Venice, only more intimate and personal, less decadent. People would often ask if Harlaxton were haunted, and paranormal study groups were always wanting to come in and spend the night to find the ghost or ghosts (I would say "No," for we were a busy, operating college, and they would have been a distraction). But in fact there was, there is, a spirit to the place, and for me it was always a benevolent spirit, a stately but kindly maternal figure. She looked after us. She taught us. She cared for us. She comforted and challenged us. She embraced us, and in turn she received our embraces.

I guess everyone has his or her special parts of Harlaxton, the places where they meet her most meaningfully. I certainly had mine: the Great Hall, of course, and the small, elegant Morning Room; the Conservatory in springtime; the Principal's Office where I worked—it had been Gregory's office, then his bedroom when he became old and ill; the little chapel at the bottom of the stone staircase, where I would stop nearly every day to offer a prayer; the Senior Common Room (Van der Elst Room), where Violet Van der Elst would call her favorite husband back to her side through séances. It wasn't because of the séances or the history or Violet that I like it: it was just an elegant room, especially after it was redecorated and updated, with its books lining the walls and its many tall windows and its warm, welcoming English-club-room feel.

Our faculty children had their special places, too, especially the secret passages; and to tell the truth so did a lot of our incoming students like those secret passages, for our grown-up students, too, had a sense of wonder that could appreciate Harlaxton's mysteries. For example, that secret doorway masquerading as a wall panel between Great Hall and State Dining Room, which opened one such passage. What an intriguing place, interesting and beckoning long after it was no longer used by the servants for whom it was created. And that corner of a wall in the Long Gallery, a secret doorway opening into a spiral staircase that extended from top to bottom of the Manor. A good mystery story could be written about that staircase and the secret doors.

If we would ever have turned Ben Baxter loose, he would have found even more secret passages—or made them! A plumber on our staff, with huge energy and an inquiring mind to go with his technical skills, he would read up on these great houses on the web, see how they were put together, and then want to explore the legends of Harlaxton: that there was a secret tunnel leading from the Music Room to beyond the great gazebos out front; that there was a huge storage area for ice just behind the giant retaining wall holding up the side gardens by the Visitors' Car Park; that there were bodies buried behind a brick wall leading from the Studio Lab to cavernous rooms underneath the garden behind the Principal's Lodge. (He did manage to break through that wall, during some repairs, and found only an old tennis shoe and maybe a tattered shirt—no bones.) Ben's curiosity is a great attribute, and we probably should have taken more advantage of it.

Or, maybe not. Maybe you can try to learn too much about the secrets of an elegant lady. Maybe we should just treat her well, listen to her sighs and night songs, appreciate all that she has been and is, and live together with her in love and care for her and for one another.

Maybe, at the end of the day, we should just treat Harlaxton Manor well.

For she has surely treated us well.

"Mrs. Culpin"

Her first name was "Mrs."

That's all I knew, for more than twenty-five years. I thought she surely must have a first name, but all she would say, all anyone would say, was "Mrs. Culpin."*

Her title was "Head Housekeeper." And she was both—a ferociously capable *Housekeeper*, and very clearly *Head*, as in, "I'm In Charge Here and Don't You Mistake It or Forget It." Not that she wasn't nice—she was always pleasant, and fun, and funny, and would go not just the second mile for you but the thirteenth or fourteenth. But she was also, always, No Nonsense about Work.

She began working at Harlaxton Manor all the way back in the Stanford University days, before Evansville was on the scene as lessee and then owner. As she told me on the phone—I called her from America to get some details for writing this sketch—Jim, her partner of now-approaching fifty years, was Gamekeeper at Belvoir Castle and the two of them were living in "that little bungalow up by the Great Front Gates of Harlaxton."

"So I just went down the lane, spoke with Professor Docker of Stanford-in-Britain, and was hired. Then the Manor was shut down for a while when Stanford moved to the Astor estate at Cliveden, and Jim had the job of looking after Harlaxton, to keep it safe and to keep the property up. Well, the University of Evansville came in, and I went down the lane again to speak with Professor Rusk, and I was hired a second time."

The stories told of Mrs. Culpin are many: of the Housekeepers coming in to the Refectory for their mid-morning break, all at the same time, and all sitting together to have their tea; of the tea break lasting exactly fifteen minutes; then Mrs. Culpin's standing up to her full height (she is all of five feet tall, maybe five-two or three—a petite and very pretty lady), and the "Housekeeping Ladies'" standing up with her, all walking out together to get back to work.

No slacking here, probably precious little time taken out for gossiping. Serious leadership, serious work.

She would knit and sew as needed for individuals and the College — drapes, clothing, curtains, whatever. She would teach students to knit and sew: "You see, they didn't know how." No kidding.

Her office, now a classroom on the ground floor and appropriately named "The Culpin Room," was a beehive of activity — ironing, repairing, making do, making clean, making whole. At end of term, when students were traveling, their "big" bags for going home to America were stashed — you guessed it — in Mrs. Culpin's office cum workroom. And if the students needed something from a suitcase at an odd hour, of course the answer was simple: up to the bungalow at the top of the lane, bring Mrs. Culpin back with her key, get what was needed, and I hope remember to say, "Thank you."

When I was a young professor teaching English at Harlaxton in 1976, Mrs. Culpin would look after any or all of us whenever the "Harlaxton Cold" would appear. There was no nurse on the staff then, and of course the "Harlaxton Cold" has been a tradition, an institution, for as long as anyone can remember. Often it was much more serious than a "common cold," for students would bring germ and virus strains back to the Manor from the four corners of Britain and Europe and beyond.

Mrs. Culpin's answer was a Special Potion, a Concoction, which she would mix up and give to you in a plain glass bottle with no label whatsoever. And it worked! I don't know what was in Mrs. Culpin's Potion, which I — a faithful and appreciative user — remember as a yellow-greenish solution filling that unmarked medicine bottle to the top. It had a kind of bittersweet taste and a real kick to it. There were rumors of a stiff lacing of codeine and alcohol, but of course students were very creative in their hopeful descriptions. Later I asked her, when I was Principal and a retired Mrs. Culpin was at an evening event at the College. I asked her what was in her medicine, what were its contents. She said she didn't remember. I'll bet!

All of this led to another rumor, of course, to the effect that the local health authorities or some shameless Principal or some other wretched person had shut down her medical dispensing business, though she never took a shilling or a pence for her concoction or for her help of any kind.

For I am here to tell you that Mrs. Culpin's medicine did the job! When I was sick, if went to her for a bottle of her Potion, and took the medicine just as she told me to do it, I was almost instantly well again. Or maybe I just felt so good from drinking her stuff that I didn't care if I was sick or well. But it worked! I wouldn't mind having a bottle tonight, right here in America.

Mrs. Culpin worked at Harlaxton from the last Stanford University Academic Director through the first three University of Evansville Principals—a space of at least twenty years, though her petite shadow seems to stretch much longer than that. No Principal has a room in Harlaxton Manor named for him, but a room is named for Mrs. Culpin!

This is right and good. "Right" because Mrs. Culpin deserves it. "Right" because to me, she stands for all those staff persons who have served Harlaxton College faithfully, year after year, generation after generation. Their names haven't been in the newspapers, their pictures weren't on television, maybe no one ever told them how important they were, but they made Harlaxton "work." They were important to every student who walked through the doors. That's why, when alumni come back to Harlaxton, they often bypass the "big" administrators in favor of visiting with a favorite British Faculty member or a member of the Housekeeping, Maintenance, or Catering, Gardens, Security, Transport, or Secretarial staff who had befriended them during their Harlaxton days.

The last time I saw Mrs. Culpin in person, probably at our Harlaxton Family Christmas where our retirees were always invited and welcomed (because, after all, they are part of the "Harlaxton Family"), she was nicely turned out in attractive holiday clothing, neat as a pin, and I asked her if she wanted a job—if she wanted to be part of our Housekeeping operation again. It was December 2013. She was nearing eighty-nine years of age, but she didn't hesitate for an instant: "Yes. I'd like to do that." I was joking, of course, and she knew it. But I'm not at all sure that she was joking. And I know in my bones that she could have handled that job or any other, very effectively. Still. Always.

Those of us who knew her, who worked with her, thought she could do *anything*.

After all, she was the one, the only, the inimitable, the indomitable, the magnificent

"Mrs. Culpin."

*"Muriel." Her first name is "Muriel."

Unlocking the Secret Rooms — and Secret Beauty — of Harlaxton Manor

When we came to Harlaxton in January 2003, it just seemed natural, as the farmers said in our small-town Missouri youth, "to git after it from the git-go." All of us know how this works: you see what needs doing, and you do your best to get it done. Now.

One thing needed, right at the start, was **a new College Plan**. Suzanne H. Kingsley was not an employee of Harlaxton College or the University of Evansville, but from her earlier experience as a Collegiate Vice President in America she knew how to do college planning. So we asked her, and she just did it, as a volunteer — saw what needed doing, and did it.

Many colleges and universities spend two or three years to get a Plan done, often with expensive outside consultants. But by the end of that first semester and summer, working with staff leaders in every department, she had drafted, and the College had discussed, and we were putting in place, a comprehensive College Plan, complete with Vision and Mission Statements and ready for Action Plans. Over several years, this Plan and its updates guided and goaded us as we improved our academic and student life programs, our staff performance and rewards, our community connections and support, and our facilities — that is, the whole bloomin' College.

We called it "Harlaxton: Pride and Purpose" — I still like the name. And the Plan said, "We know where we want to go, we have agreed on it, and we are ready to do it.'" Except . . .

Except many parts of the plan cost money, and that was in short supply both at Harlaxton and at the home University of Evansville campus. We never succeeded, for example, in getting Harlaxton faculty and staff salaries equal with Evansville faculty and staff salaries. I would like to find another way to say it, but I can't: I failed my Harlaxton colleagues as their Principal, being never effective enough to convince faculty and administrators at Evansville that equity, parity, and basic fairness were the right and moral and even sensible things to exhibit toward their colleagues, "those other faculty and staff employees of the University of Evansville over there in England."

But on some things, like our physical facilities or our technological capacities such as WiFi, individual donors from America could step in and make a huge difference. And they did. We were always careful to coordinate with Jack Barner and the fund raising office at the home campus, careful never to "take money away" from the needs at home. Fortunately, Harlaxton Manor and the Harlaxton College program were attractive to persons who could help both at home and abroad.

Suzanne had previously done successful fund raising as a Collegiate Vice President, as had I as a President. We both believed that you never tried to "talk anyone out" of his or her money, but you talked quietly with a potential donor about what Harlaxton College was doing and dreaming. If that person believed in those things, valued them, then often—when asked—he or she would invest in them philanthropically, would give money. It was a *relationship* and not just a *transaction*, a commitment that left both the donor and the College with a deep and abiding sense of satisfaction.

When I look back on it now, it is wonderful to see how good people supported Harlaxton, beginning with Dr. William Ridgway's making it possible for the University of Evansville to own Harlaxton Manor in the first place. I've made just a little list of some projects our donors accomplished in the decade-plus of our service to Harlaxton:

The Conservatory. When we arrived, the glass roof of this "green house" was all broken out. The place was derelict, couldn't be used. Rita Eykamp of the Evansville Trustees visited, said this could not be, and so she and her husband Dick gave some money and encouraged others to give some money. This giving and this energy led the University to approve use of a part of our Harlaxton surplus on the project, and the Conservatory was restored just as it had been first constructed. A secret beauty of Harlaxton was unlocked because some good people saw what needed doing and got it done.

The Bistro. What a mess *that* was! I don't remember major gifts here, but Chris Meadows and the fine Harlaxton Maintenance staff joined others to become a "design implementation team," though they wouldn't have used fancy language like that. Working together, they re-created and restored a much-used student gathering space. Needed doing. Job done.

Student Rooms. One whole corridor of student housing had been shut down because it was in such bad shape. A whole corridor! Not acceptable. Same story as above. Get after it. Make the repairs. Get good furniture. Make it an attractive place to live. And, after substantial effort, job done. God knows we needed those rooms as our enrollment grew to capacity or near capacity semester by semester.

Over the next few years, in a classic example of how it all works— (a) with financial support through gifts from former Trustee Mary Kay Powell, (b) with design and guidance from Suzanne Kingsley, (c) with leadership of a good Maintenance Team by Chris Meadows, (d) with skilled and steady work by members of that Maintenance Team—every student room in the Manor was refurbished. That's every . . . single . . . room. Chris then organized our staff so we were tending to problems as they came up instead of letting things deteriorate. Check it off. Keep it up. Job done and being done.

Faculty Offices and Library. Faculty Offices were—well, a pit. Office furniture cobbled together from hither and yon. Names on the doors in paper signs—as if each faculty member were temporary, waiting for his or her name to be ripped off the door. Just not right. So, it was made right, with nice furniture and bookshelves purchased, a coordinated décor created, and faculty names placed "permanently" on "their" doors. Dr. Edward Bujak and Dr. Sarah McKenzie pitched in and painted their own offices: the process was a sight to behold, with as much paint, it seemed, on themselves and on the floor cloths as on the walls; but the product was good! This work was important not only to make the *place* whole and attractive, but also to show respect for our *people*.

Meanwhile, the Visiting American Faculty office was moved from a remote area off the Archeological Courtyard and brought right up into the center of the academic action, next to British Faculty offices and the College Library and Seminar Room #1 — a designed concentration of both spaces and emphasis, with faculty offices, seminar room, and library all "connected" as the academic heart of the College. (The former Visiting Faculty Office in turn became a professionally furnished Studio Lab for science and art classes.)

And to complete this academic refurbishment, the very nice College Library was freshly painted, new carpeting was laid, and new furnishings purchased. Get it right. Do it right. And, mostly, just do it!

Wireless Technology. Students used to come to school with notebooks and pencils. They now come with a half-dozen electronic "devices" hanging off their ear-plugged selves, and it is essential both to their academic and their personal wellbeing that there be capacity to handle them. During an Evansville capital campaign, Trustee Chairman Alan Braun and his wife Sharon made a substantial gift that enabled wireless technology through the whole historic Harlaxton campus. It felt like, still feels like, a miracle — *that* kind of modern technology in *that* magnificent historic building. Maybe it *is* a miracle.

Faculty Flats and State Bedrooms. All were refurbished, rebuilt, newly constructed, or redecorated — whatever was needed. Mostly by our own staff. Fortunately, Suzanne had earlier worked with an interior-decorating firm, has a gift for it, and could "see" what colors and materials were needed. Always, the touchstone was "how can this space be most useful and livable." She knew, and sought to help our staff understand, that families were leaving their houses in America, their very homes, to come and live in a small flat or a single room, however grand it might be. These spaces needed to be nice, usable, practical, attractive. Over a period of eleven years, all of these were made new — every . . . single . . . one.

Manor State Rooms. We are talking here about the glory of Harlaxton Manor: the Long Gallery, the Gold Room, the Ante-Room, the State Dining Room, the Drawing Room, the Morning Room, the Senior Common Room (Van der Elst Room), the College Common Room and the Junior Common Room.

Same story. Every single room, *every one*, refurbished according to need.

These beautiful and historic rooms had last received major attention in the 1980s, during the remarkable Principalship of Dr. Graddon Rowlands and his wife Pam. They had raised "extra" money by working extra hard, alongside staff, to put on weddings, corporate events, antiques fairs, banquets, and the like; President Wallace Graves approved that money's staying at Harlaxton as an investment in improving the Manor; and the State Rooms began coming back to life.

Now, 30-40 years later, they again needed attention; and they received their just dues of refurbishment and renewal as magnificent places for students and faculty and members of the community.

I wish space and your patience would let me describe this work room by room — the careful, delicate labor that was needed, the discoveries made, the patience and persistence required. Those beautiful, historic State Rooms, the pride of Harlaxton, were now receiving the loving attention they deserved. Again, a matter of seeing what needs doing, and then getting it done. Sometimes people would object, saying things like, "But we don't do it that way." And the smiling response had to be, "We *haven't* done it that way. But *this just must be done; these rooms just must be preserved and restored.*" And they were. Every . . . single . . . room.

Schroeder Courtyard, Lion Terrace, Italian Garden. Now we are going outside and talking about some massive stone structures — the outdoor garden structures — that have deteriorated over a century and a half of buffeting by the elements. Suzanne early on began working with English Heritage and had great success in getting matching grants from them. John C. and Diane Schroeder, generous donors to Harlaxton and Evansville, as well as to other schools and causes, invested major funds to restore the historic walls and gates and stairways of the Great Front Courtyard, including two sets of the iconic Harlaxton Lions — in honor of John's father, himself a long-time Trustee of the home university and donor both to Evansville and to Harlaxton. Funds from a Worthington Family endowment helped restore the Italian Garden, as did further help from the Schroeders. Important jobs done. (Though more still to do.)

I pause here to add a brief word about the extraordinary good done by the Schroeder family at Harlaxton and elsewhere. The total of gifts made through the years by patriarch John H. Schroeder well exceeded the purchase price of the Manor. Richard Schroeder in recent years has picked up the torch of annual giving to Harlaxton by his deceased father. And year-by-year John C. and Diane Schroeder have made very substantial gifts, the largest of any ever made to Harlaxton. They have never seemed to want credit for what they do, never made a fuss about it, have seen it as something they were able to do and wanted to do so they could help students and schools and the church and other agencies in our communities, at home and around the world. Instead of looking for ways to avoid giving, they looked for ways to give to things that matter, to make a difference, to make good things happen. I often heard John say, quietly and without show, "Well, it just has to be done."

All of these projects — and when I put them all together they boggle my mind with the huge scope and scale of what was achieved — were directed toward **unlocking the secret beauty of Harlaxton by restoring and renewing places that had fallen victim to the ravages of time, either through inattention or lack of funds.** These projects were achieving what our College Plan and our aspirations promised: they were conserving the heritage that is Harlaxton Manor.

These last two projects that I now mention were able to unlock **not only secret beauties, but secret rooms, secret and unused parts of Harlaxton**. That drama is a story all its own.

The first of these is **The Harlaxton Gatehouse.** From earliest days of the Manor, the Gatehouse contained two simple flats for workers on the estate. I have even met folks, in the villages of Harlaxton and Stroxton, who lived in the Gatehouse flats as children, when their fathers worked at the Manor. Over the years, these two apartments fell into total disrepair. Some of the lead was stolen off the lead roof. The structure began to take in water and deteriorate even further. We would occasionally hear talk of "when we have to knock this building down," though English Heritage would never have permitted this historic structure to be willfully destroyed.

Enter Sharon and Burkley McCarthy, successful businesspersons from Evansville, she a University of Evansville Trustee. Sharon and Suzanne walked through the Gatehouse flats together, seeing the crumbling but historic "reed and horsehair plaster" walls covered with generations of student graffiti, looking down into the basement through the gaping hole in the floor of one flat, picking their ways through decades of rubbish and ruin, stepping carefully lest something give way and they meet with injury or worse.

And they both saw, with their eyes of purpose, not just the rubble and rubbish, not just a wrecked building, but instead they saw possibility, potential, the beauty and usefulness that could come out of these ruins. Sharon and Burkley committed a substantial gift, which was ultimately matched with a gift Suzanne solicited from English Heritage. Suzanne made charts and began considering options for layout, design, and decoration. She oversaw the project, really, from beginning to end—from dreams and design to fabrics and furniture, to carpets and colors.

With her taking the lead, our own Maintenance staff worked with the very capable Skillington Workshop and their owner Dr. David Carrington to bring the Gatehouse back to life. And on March 16, 2008, the Great Gatehouse Doors were ceremonially opened once again (we had to shut them first) and the restored building was dedicated for use—saved from dereliction and granted a new destiny. President Steve Jennings of the University of Evansville was present, as was President Gary Ransdell of our partner Western Kentucky University. So were Dr. Carrington and members of the Skillington team. And interested members of our College community. Our guests of honor, though, were the Maintenance Staff of Harlaxton College and Chris Meadows their leader, whose names are on a plaque inside the building alongside the scratched-in-plaster name of a workman who helped repair the structure in 1863. A Dream, a Donor, a Designer, some Doers. And a noteworthy, important, creative job done.

It seems all-but-incredible to me that there would be a second such project, but it happened again, in much the same way—with **Pegasus Tower**. Sharon McCarthy was visiting Harlaxton and, being pleased with the Gatehouse Project, asked if there were other spaces that could be renovated to provide income for the College (the Gatehouse flats having been leased to Western Kentucky University and to one of their Regents, John Ridley, as well as being available for professors on sabbatical leave). She and Suzanne considered the space above the archway leading to and from Manor and Carriage House, unused space in its own little mini-castle that had never been built out. Again, the McCarthys committed a major gift. Again, Suzanne went to work on design, working with Chris Meadows. And again, an apartment for guests emerged that is as nice as designer-apartments in Paris or New York or London, the creative and imaginative design being all the while totally user-friendly.

I ask myself, "How could all this happen over the period of less than a dozen years?" Largely because of two things.

First, a single person, not an employee but "a spouse," had a vision of what could be. With her passionate sense of both beauty and duty, she turned her considerable knowledge, her talents, and her intense work ethic to achieving what seemed impossible—(a) the unlocking of some secret and unused spaces in Harlaxton Manor and turning them into lodgings fit for a king or queen or professor or parent, and (b) the renewal of many spaces and rooms at Harlaxton in ways that restored not only secret beauty but also lost usefulness.

And equally important, some caring and capable donors saw the vision, gave the financial resources, and made it all happen. It could not have been done without the vision and knowledge and work of Suzanne and paid staff; and it could not have been done without the financial support of some strong and good people who caught the vision, believed in it, and *acted on their belief* in tangible, substantial ways. They gave the money!

These donors didn't owe Harlaxton anything. They gave generously because they saw, they believed, and they cared.

Suzanne didn't have a *job at* Harlaxton, wasn't required to work for Harlaxton College at all. But she also believed. She also caught, and shaped, the vision. And was willing to "git after it from the git-go."

Like a very few and special others, these people had a *calling for* Harlaxton, a *vision for* Harlaxton. And together, these donors and good staff and a gifted contractor carried that vision out to its incredible, astounding finish.

Only a few people understand this miracle of Harlaxton renewal. Those who understand it are not only astonished but also very grateful. Most others, of course, take it all for granted and in their self-centeredness say nothing, or perhaps sneer at "all that work." I'm afraid that's just the way life is.

But count me, always, as one of the former.

I, for one, am amazed at it all, astonished by what was achieved.

I, for one, am grateful.

Pigeons Pooped Here

Well, they did.

The space is now the beautiful Pegasus Tower Flat, just above the archway leading from Harlaxton's Pegasus Courtyard down to the Carriage House and Sports Hall—and back. Right next to the Principal's Lodge.

But before that Flat was created, the space was empty—as far as I know for 170 years, since Gregory Gregory built the place. It had pretty bad windows, a rotted wood floor, and for some reason a little nook of a fireplace. Clive Dowman, Harlaxton Security and Assistance officer, remembers having coffee around that little fireplace as a younger man, while warming up from sessions of beating the bushes for pheasant shooters.

But no one had ever lived in there, no offices, no classrooms, nothing. It was just empty space—except for the pigeons, which had taken it over and were very comfortable, thank you.

Now, I became interested in this extended history of pigeon-occupancy in such a prime location, and so I Googled "Pigeon" and learned that a pigeon lives from 5 to 15 years. Let's split the difference and round it off to an average 10-year lifespan, and you have seventeen generations of pigeons living there—from the most recent resident to his or her great-great-great-great-great-great-great-great-great- great- great- great- great- great- great grandfather. Now *that* is squatters' rights.

Which brings me back to the poop. Can you imagine how much of this stuff had accumulated over the century and a half plus? I mean, pigeons are not shy birds in this matter.

Well, sir or madam, along about 2010, those pigeons were evicted! As I described in the previous sketch, remarkable Sharon McCarthy and Suzanne Kingsley had the idea—a bold vision, really—to turn that space into a designer-quality apartment for professors on sabbatical leave, VIPs, and other guests — especially those who might appreciate a special kind of beauty and quality. Sharon and her husband Burkley provided money, Suzanne provided creativity, our Maintenance staff provided much of the work, and plans came to fruition that created a beautiful and livable space as good as any you can find in urban apartments costing thousands of dollars — per month.

So, of course, the pigeons had to go.

Before anything could be built, any work could be done, bye-bye birds. And not only did the birds have to go: their decades of "leavings" had to be cleaned out as well. Bye-bye poop.

I was amazed: it took a whole separate company that specializes in such things — can you imagine that as a specialty? — to clear out the 170 years of the pigeons' own creative contributions to that space. Wonder what the name of the company was.

Now and again a pigeon will come and peck at a window, look inside, and fly away in a puffed-up huff, looking for another place to leave his calling card.

Guess he hasn't heard about progress.

The Clock

It just stopped. Dead.

The giant clock in the tower at the front of Harlaxton Manor. It just stopped.

There's a lot of that going around, and so you see it a lot. On the fronts of public buildings, on churches, on schools. An historic clock stops—or maybe it was just an old clock, with not much history at all. No one was counting on it really. It was just there and wouldn't go away, like a bad habit. What was once a town's essential utility, calling people to come to work and to quit work, calling people to church or school, sounding the alarm, keeping everyone together on time and on track, had become a kind of useless eyesore, especially when it wouldn't keep time anymore, wouldn't chime anymore. And so a town, or a business, or a church, or a school would just let it sit there, its bells silent, its two hands locked in a kind of motionless sleep, telling the correct time only twice a day, and then only because it couldn't help it.

Sad, really. That what was once counted on by everyone grows ugly in its uselessness.

Well, it happened at Harlaxton. In the summer of 2006. I looked up at the clock face one morning, and nothing was moving. I listened, and nothing was sounding. My first question was "Why?" But then, with a clock that's at least 150 years old, maybe that's not even a question to ask. Maybe it was just tired and worn out.

Can't have that. Maybe other places, other people can, but not Harlaxton Manor, Harlaxton College. Because if a clock is stopped outside, in a dominant place on the front of a magnificent manor house, there exists—inevitably—the strong suspicion that things may have stopped inside as well. It is a symbolic thing, but symbol is just another form of reality. What if the workers inside stopped— or even just slacked up a little bit, "lost time," as it were. What if the students stopped studying—or even said to themselves that "close enough is okay" — a great temptation in Britain, or America, or anywhere. No, can't have that. Our steady, purposeful work is "what makes us tick," as it were.

Besides, the Harlaxton Clock is a little brother to Big Ben in London—an icon of Harlaxton, as Big Ben is of England. Can you imagine Big Ben stopping, and staying stopped? No way. Even when a Nazi bomb destroyed the House of Commons Chamber in the Houses of Parliament, Big Ben kept on telling the time, chiming the time. Through the smoke of war, the travails of peace, there she is, her hands marking the hours, her bells chiming the hours—sitting quietly reverent only for the funeral of Winston Churchill on January 30, 1965, and again for that of Margaret Thatcher on April 17, 2013.

Or go to Venice to know what a clock, a bell is all about. For more than a thousand years "Marangona," the great bell of San Marco, has tolled the hours for Venetians, warned of a fire or sounded the alarm at the appearance of an enemy fleet in the lagoon, tolled the death of a Doge, assured that all was well. It has been called "profound," "the deepest sound of Venice."

Let the Harlaxton Clock stay broken, quiet, still? No way. The sounds of emptiness would hurt too much, send the wrong messages, wound our spirits, discourage our efforts.

So what to do?

Began with Chris Meadows, our very fine Estates Manager, who knew/knows as much about that clock as anyone and who got involved in bringing it back to life—not only at this time of restoring it, but ever since. It is Chris who keeps the thing going now, who manages its temper tantrums and sulks, who figures out how to lose or gain an hour when Daylight Saving Time calls for it.

Talked with Steve Worthington, who thought the very first Harlaxton class from Evansville, who went to the Manor in 1971, might take this on as a project. He was a member of that class and proud of it. He asked around, and there was interest. Chris Weaver was very interested and made a lead gift. Others joined in. And pretty quickly we had the $25,000 needed to make the repairs.

Contacted "Smith of Derby" — a very old family firm in the town of Derby itself, 43 miles from Harlaxton, that looks after Big Ben and whose predecessor firm created the clock on the face of St. Paul's Cathedral in London — did that one in about 1705 or so. They've been around awhile. Smith of Derby had three big clocks coming in from Japan for repairs, but they thought they could get to ours right away.

Once into it, the company gave us two choices: to keep the original clockworks which "live" in their own glass-windowed room in the clock tower — marvels of jewel-like precision when they are working right, with their wheels and weights and levers spinning and humming and clicking and — well, "keeping" the time; or to buy an electronic black box that would do all of this probably more accurately without the original historic works. Both options cost about the same. I didn't talk with anyone about this except Chris Meadows, because I was afraid people would push us to give the "right" answer — that is, the most efficient, most up-to-the-minute answer. Instead, we kept the original clockworks. Some things are more "right" than "the right answer."

We did, however, agree to attach an electronic box to the story-tall wooden pendulum, that box receiving signals from an atomic clock in the town of Rugby, then adjusting the movement of the pendulum to keep the Harlaxton Clock more accurate — not totally so, for sometimes, depending on moisture and temperature, it has to "catch up." But it's pretty close all the time — just occasionally, like all of Harlaxton, "charmingly deliberate" (read "slow").

So Smith of Derby came to Harlaxton Manor, the clock was tenderly and carefully and skillfully repaired, the day came to start it up again, and behold: the pendulum swung with precision, the gears and levers moved with smooth poise, the chimes sounded out the quarter hours and half hours and hours with a graceful authority, and the historic Harlaxton Clock said to all of us on the inside and all of those on the outside what I hope will always be true of Harlaxton:

Do the work you were created to do.
Do it consistently, and accurately, and well.

Do it with style, with beauty.
Do it with authority.
In doing it, be a guide and inspiration to others.

See, it's not just an ordinary old outdoor clock that can be left to stop, and grow ugly, and be ignored, and get in the way. It's a *lesson*, and that's what Harlaxton College is all about, isn't it—teaching lessons, learning lessons. The Harlaxton Clock is a lesson in exquisite craftsmanship, a lesson in a kind of technology that is also an art, a lesson in doing our jobs in a way that all can see and be proud, can hear and be inspired.

It has to be that way. It is the **Harlaxton** Clock! On the front of **Harlaxton** Manor! Right up there above the flag of the United Kingdom of Great Britain and Northern Ireland on our left, and the flag of the United States of America on our right!

I love that clock.

Gardens and Woodlands,
Bats and Crested Newts

117 acres is a big yard.

And that's what our three "Gardeners" have to look after. That's the size of Harlaxton's property.

(Somehow it is nice that in Britain "the yard" is called "the gardens," that "yard men" are called "gardeners.")

With all this to look after, our Gardeners worked very hard during our years as their colleagues. Probably still do. Our annual staff appraisal form asked (among other things) what people liked *most* about working at Harlaxton, and what they liked *least*. One year, our very good, very hardworking Head Gardener, a man with the perfect gardener's name of Andrew Potter, wrote that what he most liked at Harlaxton was "Working," what he least liked was "Writing" — meaning, no doubt, filling out these blankety-blank appraisal forms. I'm with him! And the two other Gardeners worked hard like him, with him!

What did they do? They mowed, of course. A lot of mowing. They trimmed the large hedgerows that line the entrance lane. They tended the parts of the yards that are truly "gardens" in the American sense, though these were generally kept at a minimum because they are so labor-intensive. They looked after the plants In the Conservatory. They looked after the 6½-acre Walled Garden that once provided vegetables and fruits and flowers for the family living in Harlaxton Manor, and they turned its derelict, overrun spaces once again into lawns and an orchard and rose beds. They made woodchip trails and nature walks in the Harlaxton Woods, which at one season of the year are some of the most beautiful bluebell woods anywhere. They saw to trimming the trees, including the century-old Cedars of Lebanon that are the glory of the woodlands. They planted, they tended, they preserved, they made beautiful. Big jobs. Done well.

And then, now and again, there were complications. Might be weather. Might be staffing. Might be equipment. Or, sometimes the complications could come off the wall, as it were.

Consider this:

Britain is a country that seeks to preserve its wildlife species to an extraordinary degree, and sometimes those efforts at preservation get a little — well, interesting.

For example, bats are a protected species in Britain. We were required at Harlaxton to make little wooden bat houses for them when it was discovered that they were living in the old railway tunnel leading into the Manor and in the subspaces below the tunnel. From November to April, when the bats are hibernating, we were never, never, never to disturb them. Shhhh! Volunteer and professional "bat people" came to check — on the bats, and on us. Nice people, they are, and I hope their hearts are completely fulfilled in their line of work. There was great excitement when it was discovered that a species very rare for the Harlaxton climate — was it a White Pipistrelle, or am I mixing that up with a more common species — was hibernating in the Harlaxton Manor tunnels. Dutifully, I shared the joy.

Which is, I confess, a bit difficult for an American. When Suzanne's brother, a college professor and administrator in Birmingham, Alabama — pronounced "Ber-min-hay-yum" — had a bat roosting on the eaves of his back porch, he called the county agent who advised him to "git a broom and kill that sucker — just don't git the blood on ya 'cause sometimes they's got rabies." If the bat roosts in Birmingham, England — pronounced "Burr-ming-um" — you build a little penthouse for him, where he can sit in a little bat easy chair, wearing his little bat sunglasses, reading his little bat newspaper, listening to bat music, maybe smoking a tiny little bat electronic cigarette, checking his little bat e-mail on his little bat iPhone, and generally enjoying life as a Protected Species. If you're a bat and in America, emigrate.

So we protected our Harlaxton bats, and I learned a lot, and I really do appreciate the British care for their animal life. Most of the time.

And then there is the case of the Great Crested Newt, also known as the Northern Newt or — who slipped this debased name in? — the Warty Newt. Ugly little critters, these, about three slimy inches long. But, also, a Protected Species in the United Kingdom (and Europe as well, I think). And the Brits are serious about this little dude, too, as much as they are about their bats.

Case in point: John and Margie Histed of Dauntsey, Wiltshire, she a 68-year-old retired doctor and he a 71-year-old retired computer consultant, had their £1,000,000 ($1,600,000) house flooded when a highway drainage ditch blocked up. They spent £250,000 ($400,000) on repairs, and it flooded again. They asked the Highways Agency to unblock the drainage ditch, and the Agency refused because some Great Crested Newts had been found in the debris.

Officials then wondered if some of the teensy slimy little creatures had been washed into the Histed's house and told the couple they had to order and pay for a three-month-long survey to find out. But they couldn't even begin the survey yet, because the little newt-critters "might be breeding." Now here's this nice older couple out of their own house because newts *may* have moved in to do their sex thing!

Mr. Histed reasoned, and explained reasonably, that a very healthy colony of Great Crested Newts was living in their ten-acre pond on their property — that they weren't really anti-newt but just wanted to get back home. At last report it looked like that would not happen for at least another year, and meanwhile the Histeds are living in a camping trailer.

Well, with that lore ringing in our ears and minds, we were less than delighted when, beginning major repair work on the Lion Terrace out back of the Manor, our folks discovered a couple of Great Crested Newts. I think some were over by the Dutch Canal reflecting pool as well, but we weren't planning to work there — yet. I mentioned "serious": if you happen to kill any of the little creatures, accidentally or purposefully, you can be fined up to £5,000 per newt. *Per newt.* Zowie. So, *very, very carefully,* we created other lodgings in a nearby habitat for the Great Crested Newts — no wonder they're called "Great."

Then, of course, we had to move them into their new homes, very *carefully*. We asked them if they were satisfied, if we could do anything else for them, did they want an "A" in British Studies, or a pizza delivered, or could we go get a McDonald's cheeseburger for them and did they want fries with that. (They seemed to prefer Smartie McFlurrys. That figures.)

And then we got on with the work.

I tell these tales only to say that it is not a simple thing to be a Gardener, or a Stonemason, or a Maintenance Worker at Harlaxton Manor or anywhere else in the United Kingdom, even if you work hard and are just trying to do your job.

The bats and newts and bureaucrats are lurking.

So somebody has to have your back.

"Vision, and Courtesy, and Patience": Good Advice from Good People

In October 1988, while a Visiting Fellow at Cambridge University, I attended a "drinks party" at the President's Lodge of Wolfson College, home of my friend Professor Sir David Glyndwr Tudor Williams. David was a brilliant legal scholar who would soon become the first full-time Vice Chancellor [President] of Cambridge University, from which position he would consort with the world's great and near-great, though never losing the charming wit and humility of his native Welsh upbringing.

As a Fellow, I was doing library research on the essential qualities of effective educational leaders. And here, tonight, with some of the most illustrious leaders of Cambridge colleges present (Cambridge University being made up of thirty-one separate colleges), I resolved to "continue my research on the hoof," as it were, by asking some of these leaders to say instinctively, without advance notice or prior preparation, what qualities they saw as most important in leading a school.

I began with David himself, who swirled a drop of good whisky in his glass, thought for just a moment, then said in his soft voice: "Vision. And Courtesy. And Patience." The last two of these surprised me, though they rang true as I reflected on the college I was then leading. All three responses were quintessentially David.

Continuing through the room, I found myself with the Master of Magdalene College and asked him the same question: "What are the most important qualities of educational leaders?" Not knowing David's answer, he replied, "Vision," and then — with a chuckle — "and going to bed at ten o'clock every night." Still circulating, I posed my question to the President of Clare Hall, who said, "Vision, and" — long pause — "and there is no other."

Three heads of Cambridge colleges, three independent answers, each one saying "Vision" — and Bingo: I had a very important piece of my research not only discerned, but personified — and done.

I tell this story not only because of its intrinsic worth—it is very good information for any would-be leader, or follower, to have—but also because one of the first things I did as Principal of Harlaxton was to ask David G. T. Williams to become a member of the College Advisory Council, an offer which he accepted. (He had already helped me greatly when I was President at William Jewell, and in appreciation that fine college had recognized him with one of his twelve honorary doctorates.)

And what, pray tell, is the Advisory Council of Harlaxton College?

It is a group of English community leaders who—well, who Advise. Begun by the second Principal of Harlaxton College, Dr. Paul Bulger, in the mid 1970s, the Council advises the Principal at Harlaxton and advises the University of Evansville on how Harlaxton College can function most effectively in the British environment—remember, it is an American school on foreign soil, and most of its Principals have been American.

Examples, a tiny few among many:

David Williams was on the Academic Committee, led by Prof. John Coyne, Vice-Chancellor of the University of Derby. These two men were brilliant and flawless, particularly any time we were working with American educators. I remember a time when, at a dinner in the King's Room of Grantham's Angel and Royal Hotel, David so charmed and instructed visiting American college presidents that by the time the evening was over they were sure that Harlaxton was (a) either a secret part of Cambridge University or (b) a better school than Cambridge University. And when I first introduced John Coyne to Dr. Thomas Kazee, Evansville's president, at Langar Hall between Harlaxton and Nottingham, John's first words were, "Great win by the Purple Aces last week." He seemed to have made himself as well informed about Evansville as about Derby!

Henrietta Chubb, Chairman of the Student Life Committee (and that's the way the British say it—"chairman"—whatever the gender of the holder) and a Vice Chairman of the Council's Executive Committee, has led her Student Life group to become a significant advocate for *both* the College *and* the students, rightly seeing them as a community of shared learning and teaching rather than as adversaries.

David Armes, of our Student Life Committee and also a Vice Chairman of our Executive Committee, for over thirty years has led the brilliant Meet a Family Program, pairing our students with British host families in an experience most students rank as one of the very best in their Harlaxton days.

Dr. David Middleton of the Academic Committee has made it possible, semester after semester, for our students to hear and see traditional Morris and Clog Dancers—to experience in our own Great Hall and Conservatory and Bistro a centuries-old British folk tradition. He himself is one of the Morris Men.

Sir Simon Benton Jones has chaired a very experienced Estates Committee that has helped Harlaxton make its way through the twists and tangles of insurance, maintenance, construction, government bureaucracies, rules and regulations as we have operated and improved an historic manor house.

Sir Simon's wife, Lady Margaret—Maggie—has chaired the Advisory Council for more than twenty-five years with equal measures of grace and strength—and charm.

Mr. Robert Brownlow, also a Vice Chairman and a long-time Council member, has brought wisdom, extensive community connections, a brilliant speaking style, and a lively wit to the work of Harlaxton College. In a dozen years, I never heard a negative word about Bob Brownlow, nor did he speak ill of others.

Good advice from good people. That's what the Advisory Council is all about.

Harlaxton is indeed fortunate to hear from some of the best, in academics, in business and professional life, in community leadership, and in that centuries-old tradition of "titled" leadership, what us egalitarian Americans innocently call "the lords and ladies."

She will swim across the Atlantic and kill me for telling this; but when we were first coming to lead Harlaxton, Lady Benton Jones joined Sir Simon in hosting a dinner for us in their home, Irnham Hall. Dinners at Irnham are legendary, and though I had attended and even presided over a good number of very nice dinners in my time, this was all very different, and I was nervous. I even studied up for the occasion in an etiquette book, then had trouble remembering what I had read.

The evening came—as it always does. And now catch the scene. New Principal and wife drive to Irnham Village. They enter Irnham Manor's Great Hall, built in the 1380s. Portraits of the Benton Jones family, by generations, beam a welcome from the dark oak-paneled walls. Dining Hall beckons. Large polished table of fine wood and fine craftsmanship. Silver plates. Elegant crystal and silver cutlery in abundance. This is, as we knew it would be, no ordinary dinner.

The meal proceeds, in courses. Fine wines are poured. Poured again. Persons who would once have been called "servants" offer each dish personally from silver serving bowls. New Principal sits hoping against hope that he is doing things right. Gravy starts its way around, from hand to hand—you guessed right—in a silver gravy boat. Silver boat reaches Lady Benton Jones on my right. She pours gravy. Two drops of gravy remain on lip of gravy boat. Lady takes finger, slides gravy drops off silver gravy boat. Licks finger. No one hears Principal say, "Yes!" No one sees Principal's arms shoot into sky in sign of relieved victory. But Principal relaxes through the remainder of a warm, elegant, pleasant evening. "These impressive people," he sighs to himself, "are also good people, nice people, warm and human people."

It was only later that Suzanne reminded me, "Yes, but it was *her* gravy dish, and *her* house, and she could do whatever she wanted. You couldn't."

True enough.

But the point of these stories is that just as one of the most eminent educators in the world, Professor Sir David G. T. Williams, could speak with Presidents and Prime Ministers, Kings and Queens

(I remember his telling me once, in typical David fashion, "I hate name droppers. As I was telling the Queen last week . . . ."), he also would make the time to help the students and faculty of a very special college for American students on British soil—he cared about Harlaxton College. He was, as we say in America, "real people."

And just as Sir Simon Warley Frederick Benton Jones, 4th Baronet, and Lady Benton Jones, could preside over the historic village of Irnham and historic Irnham Hall, just as she could receive the Order of the British Empire from the Queen herself for her brilliant work in support of the British Red Cross, just as he could be High Sheriff of Lincolnshire on behalf of the Queen (the "oldest secular office under the Crown, going back to before 1066) and could serve as Chairman of the Lincoln Magistrate's Court, just as she could create a dinner or a social event that was so supremely "right" she would be interviewed on television about how to do it and asked to teach it to others, still, still, the two of them would make time to help the students and faculty of a very special college for American students on British soil—they cared about Harlaxton College. They were, as we say in America, "real people."

I count it as one the great privileges of my service to Harlaxton that I could know, and work with, such outstanding leaders as these who were also such great human beings. As my favorite poet writes it,

> Think where man's glory most begins and ends,
> And say my glory was I had such friends.

"Vision. And Courtesy. And Patience."

And if you would, please pass the gravy.

Harlaxton, Belvoir, and the Duchess

It's pronounced "Bee-ver." Not as in the French "Bel-vwah."* But "Bee-ver," like the little furry animal that builds dams.

Except it's not a furry little animal that builds dams. It's a castle. A BIG castle. About four miles from Harlaxton as the crow flies (you can see it from Harlaxton's front windows and the high ground behind the Manor). About five and a half miles by road. I should know. I've jogged it enough times, huffing and puffing, a little old bald-headed man Belvoir Castle Bound. And back.

A BIG castle, it is, and an important castle, since Robert de Todeni, a Norman noble and a standard-bearer to William the Conqueror** built the first one on the spot. Since the time of Henry VIII, it has been home to the Manners family, who have for generations held their title as Dukes of Rutland, along with tens of thousands of acres of British land — 15,000 acres around Belvoir Castle alone.

Now, why am I writing all this? Because Belvoir Castle and Harlaxton Manor share some unusual stories, as well as history. And some good moments for some Harlaxton students.

For example — and the Duchess of Rutland herself told me this tale, though in truth I had heard it elsewhere as well — it is said that Gregory Gregory built Harlaxton Manor with one room more than Belvoir Castle, in a kind of theatrical one-upmanship. (Remember, Gregory is the guy who put his name in stone letters three feet high on the front of the Manor, reading — in Latin — "Gregory Built These Buildings Perfectly." Other translations are possible, but I really like this one. If neon signs had been invented, I'm sure he would have considered that option as well.)

Even if true, that one room doesn't matter, really. It's all a game. For Belvoir Castle is colossal in size compared with Harlaxton Manor, and an extra closet or two won't change that. Belvoir is — well, a real "castle," Harlaxton just a very big manor house. Belvoir has 15,000 acres as its grounds, Harlaxton 117. There's no comparison.

(Though, to complete this part of the tale, Dr. Mark Valenzuela and some Evansville Engineering students, using state of the art borrowed equipment, proved scientifically and conclusively that the top of Harlaxton Manor is one meter higher than the top of Belvoir Castle.)

Gregory Gregory also lined up the front lane of the Manor with the steeple of Bottesford Church, eight miles away. It is a very nice architectural touch, not uncommon in creating a picturesque scene for English stately homes. But Bottesford Church also contains the tombs of the Dukes of Rutland, lying there for centuries in their cold stone armor. So, was Gregory creating an aesthetic nicety, or was he paying homage to the dukes, or was he offering a dubious salute using the Duke's own church spire?

No matter. What has really happened between Belvoir and Harlaxton, at least in the time I've known it, has been good.

Emma, the Duchess of Rutland, is a member of the Harlaxton College Advisory Council and has lent her name and nobility to Harlaxton's mission. Herself a daughter of a Welsh Quaker farming family, and an accomplished and trained opera singer (at the Guildhall School of Music and Drama in London), she knows what it is to have dreams, to work hard in achieving them, and to accomplish things you never ever even thought possible. Sound like the Harlaxton Experience?

When I asked her, she agreed and for several years invited a group of our students each semester to Belvoir Castle, ten or twelve of them at a time. It was, of course, an honor to be selected. She arranged a private tour led by Harvey Proctor, Esq., former Member of Parliament and now Private Secretary to the Duke of Rutland, and then she met with our student group privately in the family quarters of the Castle. She is an attractive woman, not one to "put on airs," and with our students was always natural and spontaneous and warm. She asked each student individually about name and hometown, asked about his or her goals in life, then encouraged each and all to seek those life goals with "determination, hard work, and joy."

It's pretty big stuff, really, when a student from an American town and an American college is invited to one of the great castles of Britain and encouraged by the Duchess herself to be the best in life that he or she can be.

Then, after this ever so exciting "audience," we would all come back to the Manor where I ordered us all some pizzas from Pizza King. You can be a lord or lady for only so long.

It was good. And I'll always remember Emma, Duchess of Rutland, very fondly. She cared for our kids, even inviting them to her big, BIG castle.

Only a Duchess could do this.

But doing this is better even than being a Duchess.

*When the Normans conquered England in 1066, they took over all the lands and castles, churches and towns. The everywhere-rulers therefore spoke Norman French, and this castle was named with the French word "Belvoir," or "beautiful view." The mostly illiterate Anglo-Saxon workers, however, couldn't pronounce the French, and so "Belvoir" became "beaver," and incredibly still is a thousand years later. There are lots of other examples: the food on the table was "venison," or "mutton" — French words; the food on the ground, as hunted or grown, was "deer" or "sheep" — Anglo-Saxon words. Language tells all.

**I've always enjoyed the fact that Duke William, while in his native Normandy, was called "William the Bastard," for he was indeed an illegitimate son of the unmarried Duke Robert I by his mistress Herleva. As if that were not enough, when he came across the English Channel to attempt the conquest of England, the first thing he did was fall out of his boat. (I think no one laughed.) The important thing, though, is not that he fell out of the boat, but that he got up again and went ashore to conquer England. And, glory be, his name was changed from "William the Bastard" to "William the Conqueror" — which goes to show, I guess, that there is hope for any of us.

The Village Church

It is a picture post card, page-of-a-calendar kind of place. You can just see the caption: "Traditional English Village Church, surrounded by Traditional English Village Churchyard."

The thing is, it is real.

A real place, with real people, and real worship.

I'm talking about the Harlaxton Village Church—properly, The Church of St. Mary and St. Peter, Harlaxton. Begun about 1174. You got that right—1174. A.D. Anno Domini.

I looked some of this up.

Harlaxton Village herself, one of England's attractive and sought after such places, is older than William the Conqueror's *Domesday Book* of 1086—his register of all the property in his English domains, done (of course) so he could collect taxes. In this *Domesday Book,* the village is called "Herlavestune," coming from the Old English "Herelaf" or the Danish Viking "Heorlaf" plus the Anglo-Saxon "tun" (meaning "enclosure, farmstead, or estate," later, of course, "town"). So, "Heorlaf's Tun." Harry's Place?

It was a relatively large village for its time, the *Domesday Book* listing seventy households—10 villagers, 2 smallholders, and 58 freemen. Sixteen "plough [plow] lands" are listed, along with sixteen men's "plough teams" and sixty acres of meadow. And two mills! Though the King had given Harlaxton to his wife Queen Edith in 1066 when he conquered the land, by the time of the *Domesday Book* twenty years later the Lord of Harlaxton was King William himself—the Conqueror.

But no church. It had no church. In fact, land was not given for a church, nor was any built, for another hundred years, when William's granddaughter Matilda made the grant. When the gift was made, and the church built, it was on the exact spot where it now sits. Talk about living history! Just walk in the door to find it.

So, on this historic spot, where a Roman villa had once stood just up what is now called Swine Hill, where Saxons and Danes and now Norman French had held control, a church was founded — Roman Catholic, of course, though in those days Rome had little to do with it, and later — after Henry VIII's break with the Church of Rome in 1534, a Protestant congregation of the Church of England.

Harlaxton Church. Both the architecture and the history of the church reflect the history of England and of Harlaxton:

In styles of architecture;

In the improvements and additions century by century (I used to give a British Studies lecture each semester on English church architecture and chose to do it in the Harlaxton Village Church — a very good move, since what we were learning from books was all around us in stone);

In the elaborate graves and effigies of the DeLignes and the Gregorys, historic Lords of Harlaxton Manor;

In the giant placards of The Ten Commandments and The Lord's Prayer up on the wall by the organ, from the time of the Protestant Reformation;

In the date "1664" and initials "WWW" carved in the soft stone behind the pulpit, quite possibly the initials of a soldier from a unit in Cromwell's army bivouacked in the church on the way to attack Belvoir Castle;

In a framed notice to the effect that "John Usher of the Isle of Ely, 1701, and Edward Deligne, Gent [Gentleman]; Natives of Harlaxton gave each of them the sum of ten pounds; the interest to be distributed yearly to the blind, lame, aged, and impotent people, and poorer widows, of the said parish" [purchasing power of those £20 today would be about £3,000 or $4,800.];

in a traditional "Mary Chapel" with an altar, also containing the roster of those killed in World War I and World War II — Harlaxton, like every place in England and Europe, lost many, sometimes most of its young men in World War I, going out from this little village to die in the trenches of Belgium and France.

And much, much more.

I've been writing about a tiny bit of the available history here, and to me it is both interesting and important. But the real story is the real story — that this is a living church today, caring for its community, including Harlaxton College and Harlaxton students and faculty, as best it can in some difficult days.

When we arrived at Harlaxton in 2003, we did what church people in America do — we "shopped around" for a "church home." We went to Grantham Baptist Church on Wharf Road, which is a fine congregation; we went to the great and historic St. Wulfram's Church in Grantham, also a worthy and beautiful place of worship; and we decided to "connect" with our local congregation in Harlaxton, partly because it seemed to "fit," and partly because of a sense that church and college could work together for the good of all.

The congregation is small — maybe fifty souls on a good Sunday. The "priest-in-charge" serves parishes in four other villages in addition to Harlaxton: Stroxton, Woolsthorpe-by-Belvoir, Denton, and Wyville-Hungerton. Church attendance in England has been declining sharply: just 10% claim they attend church regularly, compared with 40% in America — though the researchers say that the actual number attending church in both countries is less than half those numbers.

We soon observed that "Evangelism" is not an easy concept for most Church of England persons, nor is personal "Stewardship" — it is all just too "up close and personal," even intrusive, for most British persons' comfort. We talked with a local parish priest once about "visiting" unchurched people in the community, and on another occasion about conducting what seemed to us a "normal" stewardship effort of asking persons for gifts of specific amounts, according to their abilities, to get a new roof on the church. We clearly did not understand the culture, either in community or in church, for our ideas were received with genuine courtesy but also with a certain puzzlement.

And so, in this environment of decline, and without special efforts to change the trends, both church attendance and church support continue to decline.

But not the love. Not the care. That was not in decline, but was present in abundance from the Harlaxton congregation.

For example, the Harlaxton Church, every semester, conducted a Welcome Service for our students and faculty on their first weekend in England—and I don't know who was happiest, who got the most from this service, the local church folk who were offering it or our students and faculty who experienced this warm welcome in "another kind" of church. We were all being welcomed into a new country, as foreigners and strangers, but we found that "the ground was wondrous level at the foot of the Cross." Even in a strange and distant land, we were "home."

The church building was kept open every day, even though roving thieves would sometimes hit remote village churches to steal anything and everything, from lead off the roofs to gold crosses from the altar. We were invited, encouraged to come and pray, to sit alone and meditate, to find some moments with God in a place where, as T. S. Eliot wrote of the tiny village church at Little Gidding, "prayer has been valid."

From time to time the church asked me to preach, to offer the homily in their services. The central feature in Anglican [in America, Episcopalian] services is not the sermon but rather Holy Communion, and sermons are therefore about ten minutes long—which seemed to me about the right length. If you can't say it in ten minutes, you probably don't have anything to say and are just filibustering on behalf of the Deity. The church folks were always appreciative of my efforts, whether good or pitiful, even though I was a "stranger" who "preached like an American."

But the real moment of truth came when Suzanne had cancer, far, far away from the support systems of family and friends we had left behind in America. The congregation of the Church of St. Mary and St. Peter, Harlaxton, prayed for us every Sunday, Sunday after Sunday, without fail. Even now, when I see one of them, he or she might ask, very quietly and discreetly, if all is well.

We were surprised one Sunday when, in an environment of British reserve, of minding one's own business, of not encroaching or intruding on another person's privacy, a lovely woman in the congregation, who had lost her own husband to the same disease, walked right up and said "I just want you to know we are praying our knees off for you." Very un-British. Very meaning-full. Very much an act of Christian grace.

Privately, people in Harlaxton Church welcomed our students and faculty into their homes through the Meet a Family program. Members George and Christine Beesley, from their house right next to the church, welcomed our carolers to their home at every Harlaxton Family Christmas, serving hot mulled wine of George's making and delicious German pastries from Christine's own hands. "We want to help you celebrate this holy Christmas season while you are far from home." Christmas. Christian. Harlaxton Church.

Sitting here in my study as I write this, far away in America, I miss the Harlaxton Village Church—miss the ancient church building itself, miss the people who keep it alive. I miss the friendship and fellowship that was unfailingly extended, even to us rambling, roving, traveling Americans who were most unreliable in attendance. I miss the moments—too few, as I look back on it— when I sat alone in that church and found God present. I miss the holy moment in the service when the priest would say, "Lift up your hearts," and we would all respond, together, "We lift them up unto the Lord." I miss the peals of bells ringing out from tower and steeple, assuring the hearts of all, through all the countryside, that the Church was present and calling, just as God is present and calls. I miss kneeling at the altar, taking the bread from the hand of a fellow-believer, drinking the wine from a cup of hope, and murmuring "Amen."

It has all been happening in that place for over 800 years. It happens still. "Thanks be to God."

"We'll Leave the Light On for You"

"I'm Tom Bodett for Motel 6, and we'll leave the light on for you."

We used to hear it in America, before we went to Harlaxton in 2003 to, as they say it, "take the helm." It is one of America's most successful ad slogans, ever. And I liked it. And I liked Tom Bodett. Sounded down home, folksy, like the sort of person who would stay at a Motel 6.

Well, if Harlaxton Manor is anything, it is *not* a Motel 6! All the magnificence, all the glory, all the permanence, all the rich decor, all the high ceilings and tall windows and marble and gold decorations and silk wallpapers and — well, just plain old Grandeur. Last thing I heard there were 153 rooms in Harlaxton Manor, but who really knows. And who's counting. No Motel 6 here!

And now the ironies begin: as we got into the work at Harlaxton, it was pretty clear that the folks who come to magnificent Harlaxton Manor to do what Harlaxton College now does — the students, the faculty, the visitors, the alumni — are *not* pseudo-elegant types who put on airs, but are mostly Tom Bodett kinds of folks.

Born in Champaign, IL, grew up in Sturgis, MI, then to Oregon after a "failed student career" at Michigan State. "Being a knucklehead was a lifestyle choice." Hitchhiked to Alaska and began building houses and doing odd jobs in little Homer, Alaska (population 5,000). As he later said it, "I never remember deciding to stay. I just kept not leaving. Having bear and moose in the yard and eagles on the roof was peculiar at times, but you get used to that." Started doing some pieces for the local National Public Radio station; some of them made their way up to the national program "All Things Considered"; and then it happened: "one day a guy named David Fowler, a creative director from the Richards Group advertising agency, was driving down the Dallas Parkway in his pickup truck listening to the public radio station his receiver had been stuck on for months. Suddenly a homey voiced monologue emerged from his dusty dashboard.

He heard the name, Tom Bodett, and thought, 'Gosh, if I only had an account for a national budget motel brand with a sense of humor and humility, I could make a heck of an advertising campaign with this guy.' Enter Motel 6, and the rest, as they say, is history." The "We'll leave the light on for you" was an ad-lib by Tom Bodett, one of the most fortunate ones ever dropped.

So there it was, not really in my head but in my instincts, my intuitions, my sense of who we were and where we were. Down-home, Tom Bodett kinds of folks, coming from America to live and work and study in one of the hundred best stately homes in England [see Simon Jenkins of the London *Times*], in gloriously splendid Harlaxton Manor. As if we were all suddenly transmuted into lords and ladies.

"College in a Castle," it was. It really was. But really, down deep, we were just folks.

It is one of those choice ironies that most British people and American academics love. That **Us's** would be **Here**!

Add to that the hospitality. Whatever else you may say about Harlaxton, everyone agrees it is a friendly kind of place. Americans are by nature friendly, but so are our all-British staff—who, in modern multicultural Britain, may come from the village next door or from another continent! Together, American residents and British staff perpetuate the historic and legendary hospitality of great houses like Harlaxton Manor.

So there it all is: good ole down-home American folks, living in a stately English manor house, where American and British people alike offer a sincere hospitality. Rich ironies, warm truth.

And so my fingers on their own began signing e-mails and reports to our home and partner campuses, or notes to past or prospective guests, or e-mails to alumni, with the words, "Come when you can. We'll leave the light on for you." Or sometimes, when I credited the recipient with a good sense of irony, "We'll leave the light on for you at our l'il Motel 6."

I don't know if anyone ever "got it." No one ever talked about it.

But I did. I "got it."

And I still think it "got" Harlaxton.

A postscript: I wish Tom Bodett could have come to Harlaxton to relish these ironies—though I guess I never asked him. After nearly twenty-five years in Alaska and a rich career in radio, writing, and voice acting, he moved to "the middle of a hayfield" in Vermont where he writes books and stuff "in the barn, over his woodshop, looks for things to do with a small tractor, and keeps a small studio."

Grantham, Isaac Newton,
and Maggie Thatcher

I like Grantham.

An old draggy market town of about 40,000 souls, it is. About four miles from Harlaxton's front door. The place where our students and faculty would catch their trains to the world. I like it.

The town takes a lot of abuse in chatter and press, it may be needing a clearer civic vision, it is sort of hemmed in by the bigger shopping towns of Nottingham, Lincoln, and Peterborough, and it is — well, an ordinary kind of place. But I like it. It feels to me like what it is: an historic English market town, with a High Street that leads out to London in one direction and out to Edinburgh in the other. If Grantham is not going anywhere, its High Street surely is!

The town once won a dubious award from a national newspaper as "the most boring town in England." I gather that an entrepreneurial local hotel did pretty well by packaging "Boring Weekends" in response, encouraging stressed-out Londoners to get away from it all.

And a poet friend says that when he goes to Grantham all he sees on the streets are sixteen-year-old girls with cigarettes in their mouths and babies on their hips or old people running folks down on the sidewalks ("footpaths," "pavements") with their little electric go-cart scooters — which the National Health Service provides free when people need them. Apparently a lot of people do "need" them.

I don't care: I like Grantham.

I like The Angel and Royal Hotel, where it is said that seven Kings of England have stayed (actually, I think they snuck in Oliver Cromwell). I like it that The Angel sees and bills itself as "England's Oldest Inn" (dating back to c. 1203, when it was a hostel for the Knights Templar) and still retains the stable doors where horses were kept when it was a stagecoach stop on the Great North Road, still uses the large "King's Dining Room" upstairs where King John and later King Richard III held court.*

I like The George across the High Street from The Angel, formerly a hotel and now an indoor shopping center, where Thomas Paine once lived when he was a tax collector for King George III, before he changed his mind and moved to the American Colonies and wrote pamphlets that George Washington had read to his troops, helping inspire them to victory in the American Revolution.** Charles Dickens, too, once came along by stagecoach and stayed at The George (though it seemed to be stretching it a bit when in 1976, the year I first taught at Harlaxton, a billboard quoted Dickens's praise of The George Hotel as an endorsement—made you feel like maybe they hadn't changed the sheets since Dickens slept there on January 30, 1838).***

One section of The George, now a pizza place, was an apothecary's shop (drug store) in 1655 when a twelve-year-old Isaac Newton came in from the country, ten miles away out at little Woolsthorpe Manor, worked in the shop, lived with the owner's family, and attended The King's School. Just a dozen years later, Newton had made such startling scientific discoveries that the poet Alexander Pope would be inspired to write this couplet, intended ultimately as Newton's epitaph:

Nature and Nature's laws lay hid in night:
God said, "Let Newton be!" and all was light.

I like the Costa coffee shop, in the Isaac Newton Shopping Center, where I would sometimes sit sipping a Medium Americano with hot milk, eating a blueberry muffin, and pondering the statue of "Newton" across the High Street—the base of the statue didn't need to say anything else—just "Newton." I would marvel at how greatness can come from the most humble beginnings.

I like Isaac Newton's school—the original stone schoolhouse Newton attended before going on to Trinity College, Cambridge, as a "sizar" — a kind of work-study student. There his little schoolhouse stands, still, with "I. Newton" still carved in the soft stone of a window ledge, marking a stage in the life of one of the greatest scientists the world has ever known. (My son Craig, who attended The King's School in 1976 while I was teaching at Harlaxton, once asked his headmaster if he might carve his name in the stone as Newton had done. The headmaster, with the starchy and headmasterly name of R. M. W. Farden, gave the perfect headmasterly response: "Young man, when you have accomplished what Mr. Newton accomplished, we will invite you back to carve your name in our stone.")

I like the simplicity of Maggie Thatcher's girlhood home, a little red-brick cold-water flat above her family's little corner grocery store, where she worked alongside other members of her family. On Sundays she would attend the Methodist Church, where her father was a lay preacher (as well as being mayor of Grantham, not because he was high class but because he was reliable and honest). On weekdays she would attend the Kesteven and Grantham Girl's School (locally, "KGGS") as a star Chemistry student and Head Girl, then got a scholarship to Oxford, which allowed her to keep studying Chemistry. Except that she also got involved in student Conservative Party politics at Oxford. And the rest, as they say, is history.

I like it that Maggie Thatcher's girlhood flat is scarcely a ten-minute walk from the place where Isaac Newton lived when he went to school in Grantham. I know. I've walked it.

So, I like Grantham. It whispers its history, very softly. It breathes the real lives of real people. It doesn't try to be something it isn't. It just trudges on.

And, now and again, a young person who will become the greatest scientist in the world walks its streets and goes to its church and attends its school and works in one of its shops,

And a couple of centuries later another person who will become England's only woman Prime Minister ever, and one of the nation's most effective leaders ever, walks the same streets and goes to a nearby church and a nearby school and works in a nearby shop,

And they probably both agreed in their own days and ways with the newspaper that would one day call Grantham the most boring town in England,

But somehow, somewhere, a spark was lighted, and a fire burned,

and behold, God said let Newton be Newton,

and behold, God said let Thatcher be Thatcher,

Even in Grantham.

Ho hum.

*It gets even better. According to The Angel and Royal Hotel, when Prince William received his pilot's wings at nearby RAF Cranwell, the British "air force academy," in 2008, The Angel and Royal Hotel played host to a very special guest: a young lady known back then simply as Miss Kate Middleton. Arriving late on a Sunday evening, the future princess impressed the staff with her total lack of airs and pretentions. Seeing the restaurant was closed and the tables already set for breakfast the following morning, she asked for just a bowl of cornflakes—and munched on her impromptu snack in the Reception area before heading up to her room. For "The Angel," it is "The Saga of The Princess and the Cornflakes."

**Thomas Paine, a troubled figure whose Quaker leanings and personal truculence fought for supremacy in his soul, lived in Grantham and collected taxes for the King between 1762 and 1764. He ultimately moved to the American Colonies, encouraged by a London meeting with Benjamin Franklin, where he joined a printing firm in Philadelphia, wrote articles against slavery and against the inferior status of women, and in 1776 wrote *Common Sense,* a tract which — astoundingly — was read by a larger percentage of the population than today watches the Super Bowl. That pamphlet is credited with helping change a simple revolt of "aggrieved Englishmen" into a revolution, a war of independence for a new country of "free Americans." When George Washington had the pamphlet read to his troops as inspiration, Thomas Paine was himself one of those troops serving in the Continental Army; and in that same year of 1776 he wrote another inspirational tract, *The Crisis,* with its memorable opening lines, "These are the times that try men's souls." After independence was won in America, he served the cause of liberty in the French Revolution, wrote *The Rights of Man* and *The Age of Reason,* was accused with some validity of religious heresy and political treason for his extreme views, and ultimately was rejected by all and buried in an unmarked grave, its location unknown. It was a long and tortured journey from Grantham, but along the way Thomas Paine had become a true hero of American independence.

***Dickens mentioned "The George Inn" in his novel *Nicholas Nickleby,* published in March, 1838, calling it "one of the best inns in England."

Shopping: The Better Mousetrap, and Bagging the Goods

I'm sorry to tell you that the consumer service economy is not well developed in the United Kingdom.

Some have it down pat, to be sure—I think of McDonald's, of course, and the brilliant British firm of Specsavers. But by and large, if you are shopping in Britain you are on your own with little or no help from the people in the stores. Which is difficult to understand in such a courteous country.

Example #1: We needed a mousetrap. Harlaxton is set in 117 acres, much of it woodlands, some of the woodland backing right up on the Principal's Lodge. Winter was coming, and we had a sudden cold snap. Predictably, little meeses began sensing the warmth of the house and coming inside. We didn't much want to share our kitchen with mice, and so off we went to town—to buy a mousetrap. Sounds simple enough.

I asked around. "Try Homebase (a kind of Home Depot for Britain). They have everything. " And they do—occasionally. After a thirty-minute search to find the right area of the big store and to find the right shelf, there it was: the Mousetrap Section. Empty. Bare.

Time to ask for help.

"Oh, yes, we stock mouse traps, but only three or four at a time. A big lorry is coming up from London tomorrow, though—it may have some on board." None of that computed very well: little mice, little mousetrap, big lorry, but only three or four traps at a time?

"Could you recommend a place where we might find a mousetrap right now?"

"Oh, maybe try Poundland or Wilkinson's in the Isaac Newton Centre. They have lots of bits and bobs."

Onward to the Isaac Newton Shopping Centre to check out these two stores. Yes, lots of bits and bobs. But no mousetraps. Each store was willing to send us elsewhere, and then others to other elsewheres, until we had been to six separate stores in search of a simple entity that apparently did not exist in Britain. A mousetrap. And all the while, the little mice were back at our house, putting on their pajamas and settling in, chuckling a bit at these humans who would be so foolish as to seek their demise.

At the last no-mousetrap stop, we were referred to—now get this— a pet shop. "But we don't want to turn them into pets; we want to kill the little wretches." Long look of disapproval down a long British nose, for we were bespeaking "cruelty to little animals." The "wretches" were clearly not the mice, but the cruel Americans. You've seen their movies, haven't you? Lots of guns and killing.

Well, with small hope remaining in our hearts, we dutifully trekked to the pet shop, located across from Pizza Hut and McDonald's in Grantham, in one of those nice historic little buildings now spoiled by some giant ugly plastic-looking gray monstrosities stuck in next door—how did those things, which currently dispense beauty supplies, ever get approval from the Planning Authority. No doubt part of a well-studied Uglification Campaign.

Whatever—we slunk into the pet shop, told the manager our mission, and he immediately said, "Of course, I can help." He reached into a hidden shelf inside a cabinet—very hush hush like— and pulled out, I lie not, a kind of plastic penthouse for mice, with separate rooms and what looked like a kitchen, and no doubt a private bathroom with hot and cold running though slightly mousey water. Okay, it wasn't quite that bad, but still I could just picture the little critters putting on their little mousey bathrobes, picking up their little mousey telephones, and inviting all their little mousey relatives from the Balkans into the Kingsley flat "where the livin' is good."

Again, I say to the manager, "But we don't want to turn them into pets; we want to kill them." And again, a look of scorn from the manager: "Well, you could just catch them in this mouse house, then take them outside and let them go. No need to destroy them."

Unspoken were his final words, "You American butchers."

I knew better. Professor Bujak had told me he had trapped the same mouse sixty-eight times, letting him loose out back and welcoming him in again the next morning. He had even marked that mouse so he would know him, and he had named him Uber-Mouse. I gathered they had become good friends.

So, we just went home, and I resolved to order from Amazon.co.uk a teensy little gun and teensy little bullets, which I would shoot at the teensy little mice.

Didn't have to, though: it turns out that Pat, the Harlaxton Gardener, had some mouse traps of the kind we knew and loved — the ones where you set peanut butter or cheese on a little plastic shelf, the mouse comes to nibble, and SLAM — a spring releases a metal snap-trap that sends little mousey souls to a little mousey heaven. She gave us some of these traps, and with this superior technology victory was secured. Until the next cold snap when more mousey kinfolk invaded.

Or, Example #2: over the years Suzanne purchased, on behalf of our Harlaxton Housekeeping Team, literally hundreds, maybe thousands, of towels, sheets, pillowcases, duvets [down comforters] and other household goods from the Grantham branch of a leading British **"homewares and soft furnishings** store" — a huge, highly-respected organization. This is no shabby store, and this is no shabby customer dropping in for a toothbrush!

Trouble was, the salespeople in that establishment apparently found that customers were a bother, interrupting their chatting and their fondling the merchandise under the guise of straightening it up.

So, more than once, Suzanne would wheel a loaded cart or two up to the checkout stand, would cough demurely or clear her throat or say "Excuse me" in an effort to get the attention of a checkout clerk who was chatting away with her gossiping mates. Then she would patiently stand there until a clerk deigned to notice her.

With a sigh — because handling all this merchandise was a bother, you know — the clerk would slowly, with pained expression, come to the counter, where she would slowly ring up each item and drop it into a disorderly mass on the counter. Suzanne would then sign a credit card slip for a purchase in the hundreds of British pounds.

And then the clerk would sigh again and ask, glumly, "Do you want all that in a bag?"

Now how could Suzanne answer that? She always forbore responding, "Oh, no, I'll just take it out to the car one item at a time and pitch it in the back." Instead, she would smile and say, "That would be nice." And wearily, grumpily, the clerk would stash the stuff in bags for Suzanne to schlep out to the vehicle. No words of "Thank you," no "Come again," no "We appreciate your business." Just another sigh and a return to her riveting conversation.

I concluded, after accompanying Suzanne on one of these forays to this branch of this much-respected chain, watching good College money go into its coffers, that this outfit has good stock but is in serious need of a training program for staff — or of new staff who can somehow find it in themselves to be civil and helpful.

I also concluded that America is in no danger of being overtaken by Britain in retail salesmanship.

The fact is, Britain is a lovely nation of lovely people. She is rich in history, in culture, in support of theatre and the arts, in protecting the environment and green spaces. I like the country, I like the people, and I might even choose to live there if I didn't have to support not one but two of the world's great democracies with my personal income taxes. (And that's another story.)

But thank God for online shopping.

If you are going to be treated as "not there," you might as well not be there.

"You Want a Box for That?"

It was happening before we left America for England twelve years ago, but by the time we came back it was an institution. You can't go into any restaurant of any kind in the good ole U. S. of A. without seeing, tucked over in the place where servers figure out the bills, a big stack of Styrofoam boxes for customers to haul away the drippings and leavings and residues of their feast.

I mean, it's not enough any more to pig out and grow fat. We have to pig out some more the next day and grow fatter on the same food, in the process strewing Styro boxes across all amber waves of grain and purple mountain majesties above the fruited plain.

America! America! Though God sheds his grace all over thee, he must be disappointed in those boxes.

Before we left England to come back home, we were seeing a few hints and signs here and there that the Brits were catching on to this nonsense. Oh, to be sure, they still aren't camping on you while you eat, the server first telling you all bubbly and enthusiastic "that's my favorite dish" ("Frankly, my dear, I don't give a d−n"). Nor are they thumping the check down next to your left pinky before you can even ponder the dessert menu. Nor are they trying to evict you so they can turn your table over a couple of more times before 9:18pm−shoot, a lot of English diners aren't even coming in until then. Brits still eat civilized.

But this American corruption of the Styrofoam boxes, like so many others, is grunging its way into a few places. Mostly because visiting Americans are asking for it.

A friend told me a delightful story on this very point−he swears it is true and that he witnessed it, and he even gave me the names (which I have of course mercifully forgot). It happened at the Blue Pig Pub on Swinegate in Grantham, an historic hostelry where workers stayed when they were building St. Wulfram's church in the 1200s, maybe earlier. And where some Harlaxton folks like to eat now. And this example of "customer service," which I am about to narrate for you, gives a singular lie to my earlier rant about shops not being helpful in Britain.

Here is the drama: Meal finished. American asks if he can take remainder of meal home with him — "home," in this instance, being Harlaxton Manor for this visiting professor. The waiter, who is also the owner, seems confused, but keeps his cool and murmurs "Of course, sir." Long wait, as a rare moment of "British customer care" organizes itself. Sounds of dishes and silverware come from the kitchen, not the ordinary sounds but more like a moving van at the back door. And finally the owner/waiter emerges with two huge brown paper bags, like grocery bags used to be, both of them packed full and neatly with the leavings of dinner. At one glance you know it will take two men and a small boy to get all this to the car. And you wonder how the leftovers from a single meal could fill two bags.

And then, still puzzled, the owner/waiter asks, politely if not plaintively: "Sir, could you bring the crockery and cutlery back to the pub when you are finished with it?" He was sending, as carryout, the dishes and silverware along with the food!

God Save the Queen!

The Pheasant Shoots

That's "pheasants," not "peasants." Peasants were shot in an earlier century of British history. (Pheasants, too, for that matter.)

And that's "shooting," not "hunting." They're different things.

The "Harlaxton Pheasant Shoots" happen every year on selected Mondays, in season, from late October to mid-January. Harlaxton College doesn't possess the "shooting rights" to its own property — the Jesuits sold these rights separately when Harlaxton Manor and its 117 acres of mostly-woodlands were purchased in the 1980s. The shooting rights went to a "syndicate" of local persons, led by our very nice neighbor farmer John Madge.

The "shoots" themselves, like many things in Britain, are much ritualized, almost ceremonial. The "shooters" stand just so, the dog retrievers are handled just so, when needful the bushes are beaten just so to drive the pheasants out into the open, and all is done with a certain rugged form.

The pheasants themselves are raised in pens in Harlaxton Woods. Fed by a gamekeeper, David Madge. Watered by him. Looked after by him. Not that I know anything about it, but sounds to me like the birds would be almost tame when they are released to be — well, "harvested." Release from the pheasant pens means freedom in the woods and hedgerows — we would hear them a lot at night from open windows in the Principal's Lodge, along with sounds of owls and other night birds. The occasional one would fly over a high wall and into our back garden.

Once released, the pheasants are bothered by no human until they reach a certain age and size, when they are eligible for what the shooters see as "sport" — not sure the pheasants share that view. In fact, in a nation known for its sense of good sportsmanship, I've always thought this pheasant shoot thing was a little stacked against the birds. (Though, I guess, if you think of it as raising meat for the table, the pheasants have a better chance of it than pigs or cows or lambs.)

A very good Monday shoot at Harlaxton yields 50-60 or so birds for the shooters, and of course there is spirited competition among shooters to bag the most birds and a cash "pool" on how many birds the entire group will get.

In earlier days, a ceremonial tradition was to leave two of the first birds killed on the doorstep of the Lord of the Manor—you can imagine the surprise of Suzanne and me when, on one of our first Mondays at Harlaxton, we found two dead birds tied together—is that called a "brace of pheasants"?—lying on our front stoop. I guess we were as close to lord and lady as they could find at Harlaxton, which shows how precipitously the higher orders have fallen. Immediately on seeing the birds lying there, and with that sense of firm but calm authority I always exuded as Principal of Harlaxton College, I bellowed out "Whazzat?" We ended up taking the birds across to Tony Sheridan in Catering who made quite a good meal of them—pheasant meat, prepared well, is very tasty.

All this shooting is going on, of course, while students are in their classes at Harlaxton or making their own ways around buildings and grounds between or after or before their classes. Since there is *not* a whole lot of pheasant shooting going on at most American colleges and universities, the "pop-pop" of shotguns is at times a bit puzzling, if not disorienting or unnerving, to our American students and faculty—despite advance notice that the shoot would be happening.

To be sure, the "shooters" are very careful, and their ritualistic approach to the sport doesn't allow free-lancing in the aiming of their guns, and there has never ever ever been an accident. But still the first Harlaxton Pheasant Shoot of the season unfailingly elicits a hoary line of caution that successive Deans of Students have used with successive generations of their charges:

"Don't go into the woods today.

"Especially if you are dressed like a pheasant."

Ridley

I lie not. This really happened.

I was working one September night at my desktop computer in the Principal's Lodge, looking out onto Pegasus Courtyard, when the phone rang. I picked it up.

"Hello?" said I.

And in an authoritative but sort of Southern (US) tone, the voice at the other end of the line said,

"Hello. This is the Governor of Kentucky. I am sitting here at The Feathers Pub in Woodstock, and they have 200 brands of gin here, and we're doing the best we can but are only at 74 or 75. Could you come and help us?"

Now how do you respond to that?!! Remember, I am in the Principal's Lodge at Harlaxton College. Dry campus, so to speak. In England, not America, certainly not Kentucky. And some guy calls saying he is the Governor of Kentucky and giving me some story about acres of gin seventy-five or eighty miles down the road at Woodstock, next to Oxford.

But then it hit me. And I said,

"You wouldn't be a Governor of Kentucky being led astray by your cousin, would you?" Some ugly little fellow named John Ridley, who specializes in getting Governors in trouble, especially when they are visiting England?

And a great roaring laughter welcomed my response.

For it really *was* the Governor of the Commonwealth of Kentucky, Steve L. Beshear. And he really *was* at The Feathers in Woodstock, right next door to Blenheim Palace, where his daughter was a competing rider in the Blenheim International Horse Trials on the next day.

And his cousin, my friend John Ridley? He is also a friend of Harlaxton College and of half the people in Harlaxton Village, probably half the people in the world? John's wife Carolyn told me once that "other people collect stamps or coins; John collects people."

What a wonderful man and character John is! Born and raised, like "my cousin, the Governor," in Dawson Springs, Kentucky (formerly "Tradewater Bend" — Town Motto: "A Very Special Place" — population in 2010 of 2,764), John like his cousin Steve Beshear moved on, even while keeping deep roots in his home town. The Governor is, for now, in Frankfort, KY, the state capitol. John is in Bowling Green, KY, where he majored in Biology at Western Kentucky University, operated his own business for some years — a plant nursery — then for the past twenty-five has been in the financial services business, presently as Managing Director of his own Wells Fargo Advisors Financial Consulting Group in Bowling Green. He is very good. I'm a client, and I know.

We met John and Carolyn at Harlaxton, when they came over to visit a very fine Western Kentucky student whom they had "rescued" financially at the last minute, making it possible for her to come on to Harlaxton instead of dropping out. She is not the only student they have helped! We hit it off, and our personal friendship, as well as John's friendship with Harlaxton, has grown only stronger.

Wherever John is, he is involved. For example,

> He comes to Harlaxton, and he brings his gardening tools so he can help out somewhere.

> He watches a local farmer planting seed potatoes in the field in front of Harlaxton and asks if he can ride the potato planter for a few rows, just to see what it is like. He does, plants four rows, and later I ask the farm hand how John's potatoes are doing. With a wink the fellow answers, "His are the only four rows NOT growing — the rest of the crop is doing fine." You can imagine how much I enjoyed passing on *that* piece of information to Farmer Ridley.

He buys into the local "syndicate" that conducts the Harlaxton Pheasant Shoots, learns the ceremonial ropes, in the process making even more friends; and he is proud as can be that in November 2014 he sets a record for pheasants bagged in a single "shoot" – I think he bagged fifteen of the seventy-six birds, "a great day . . . a record for the day." And typically, John wrote afterwards that "Les Johnson [one of the Members] said to me that I had been invited to join the syndicate only if I pointed at the bird, shot and missed, leaving the sport to him and the English shooters." Good British humor, good international friendship.

One year, we went together to the Chelsea Flower Show in London, where John the old nursery man and Suzanne the skilled gardener not only had a fine time, but also taught us slackers a few good lessons about plants and beauty.

John wanted to go to Normandy, to see the landing beaches, and so we went, along with a lawyer friend. I had been many times, but this one was different: John wanted to learn in depth about it all, and he hired as a guide Gary Weight, another friend of Harlaxton who has made it his life's mission and business to guide persons through the solemn splendor of the American Cemetery high on a bluff over the Atlantic and along the landing beaches themselves. Gary is a superb guide: he chose an overcast day much like it was on D-Day, June 6, 1944, and took us to Omaha Beach as the tide was coming in – just like on D-Day morning itself. He drew with a stick, in the packed wet sand, the positions of the Germans, the assault waves of the Americans, and had us so engrossed in the drama that we barely got off the beach before the tide engulfed us – which was, of course, Gary's plan. As I say, I had been on that beach many times, at that cemetery many times, but through John's magic and curiosity this one made it all especially real.

John knows almost all the staff of Harlaxton College, and they know him. When John is coming to town, there is a certain eager anticipation, a certain pleasure in the air. They know that John likes them, and that when he is around good and interesting and fun things happen.

But back to "my cousin, the Governor." Awhile back, John took us to the Kentucky Derby, where we watched the races in a style we would like to become accustomed to — in a giant glassed-in skybox, with food and drink galore. Who even cared about them 'orses!

And as part of the weekend, he took us to the Governor's Mansion for the Derby Eve Gala Ball, where just three hundred guests were invited. This man has style. "My cousin, the Governor" very skillfully showcased Kentucky products in the food and drinks that were served, leading one guest to say, "We're so lucky to have a governor in office who understands farming and distilleries and the importance of these to this state. He comes from farm people, good people. He gets it." I tell you, with this kind of talk, "My cousin, the Governor" can win elections in Kentucky forever!

I told John after that weekend that I now expected, whenever I drive across the Ohio River bridge from Indiana into Louisville, to see on the big welcome sign not "Steve L. Beshear, Governor," but instead, "My Cousin, the Governor — Forever. Signed John Ridley."

John, the Biology major, is now one of eleven Regents [Trustees] of Western Kentucky University, Harlaxton's main Partner College. He, like his college fraternity brother and good friend, WKU President Gary Ransdell, is a great supporter of Harlaxton. The University leases the apartment on one side of the Harlaxton Gatehouse for use of University staff, donors, and VIPs, styling it a part of "WKU in England." Regent John Ridley leases the other side, using it on his frequent visits to Harlaxton, and making it available to clients, family, and friends. When John is not using it, he encourages Harlaxton to rent it out: "That way, you get a 'toofer' — my rent, and the guest's — to help Harlaxton students."

I don't know if the Governor and his cousin and family and friends drank all 200 brands of gin that night at The Feathers Pub in Woodstock. I don't know if they drank any at all. But I do know that they are good people, doing important and good things, along the way living life to the full.

And I know that John Ridley, a good man, is my friend.

Those Other Harlaxton Alums

We often welcomed alumni back to Harlaxton, some with boy friends or girl friends, some with wives or husbands, some with children. It was very satisfying to chat with them, to see the "Harlaxton Look" in their eyes, to hear them remember and reflect on how "Harlaxton changed my life."

Almost all of these alums, those I met in the Principal's Office, were semester students from the years when Harlaxton has been "the British campus of the University of Evansville," that is since 1971.

But there are other alums.

By far the largest in numbers are those persons who have come to Harlaxton for "summer school." A small five-week program in early summer is organized by the University of Evansville, featuring up to six courses and often enrolling students from other colleges and universities as well as "UE." And then for the remainder of the summer, all kinds of groups from all kinds of schools—a seminar in Business from the University of Evansville; programs in Business and Sociology and Nursing from Marian University in Indianapolis; a "Literary Landscapes" course from Eastern Illinois University; a near-identical course, taught by a former EIU professor, from Arizona State University; a summer intensive science course with students from Gatton Academy, a science and math high school located on the campus of Western Kentucky University which for the last three years has been named the best high school in the United States; multiple courses from Florida Southern College, who have come to Harlaxton in summer for more than thirty years; an exciting literature course from the College of New Jersey; a large and lively "elderhostel," called in Britain "The University of the Third Age," that fills the Manor; a Harlaxton Symposium in Medieval Studies that attracts some of the best scholars in the world and issues an annual volume of academic papers; an always-creative seminar in religion and literature from Western Kentucky; Comparative Health Systems courses from Evansville that draw an international audience; and on and on. Some are regulars, some are "here this year, gone next year," but it is all a lively and heady brew presided over by Harlaxton's Manager of Programmes and Events Simon Hawkes. From Europe and Britain and America they come, sometimes from the Middle East and Far East, and each one makes a claim on Harlaxton, is claimed by Harlaxton, becomes a Harlaxton "alum."

And then there is Stanford. In the 1960s Harlaxton Manor was "Stanford in Britain," one of the early overseas campuses from any American university. Both students and faculty came from Stanford University of California—officially, the "Leland Stanford Junior University." During my time as Principal, alumni from those Stanford years would sometimes hold reunions at Harlaxton in the summer, and a few would drop in at other times of the year. Their shared photographs at these reunions were a hoot: here were distinguished doctors and lawyers and professors and businessmen and women, now mature in years, pulling out photos of themselves when they were long-haired hippie types. Once upon a time they were raising hell and saving the world from the grownups, all the while achieving brilliant things academically and turning themselves into those grownups in charge of the world. The laughter at these events was uproarious, the memories warm and rich.

Even before Stanford, and just after World War II, the Jesuits owned Harlaxton Manor and conducted two programs simultaneously: a retirement home for elderly priests, who had a marvelous job description—"To Pray for the World"; and a novitiate for boys of age 14 or so, a program of study and prayer and contemplation to determine if these lads had a "call" to seek ordination and enter a life as a Jesuit priest. Over the years, I met three of these persons, one having gone on to take holy orders as a Jesuit priest, two having left before taking vows, but all shaped in different ways by their own "Harlaxton Experience."

"John S." became a good friend and continues so. He has showed me where his "cell" was, in what is now the Principal's Lodge—the place where he slept and studied. He has told me what life was like for the young men—the readings during meals in the Refectory, from the Bible or Ignatius Loyola or devotional treatises (he even showed me where the readers stood while offering this spiritual food to complement the Spartan meals), their few free hours, the strictness of their schedules. He has told me of discipline by the Jesuit priests, and the hours of instruction. John ultimately left the priesthood and found a worthy calling in the profession of books and writing — founded the Puffin Book Club of children's books for Penguin, owned and operated several book stores in the Oxford area, and more recently has written books on spirituality and on the silent order of Carthusian monks. He remembers Harlaxton fondly, visited from time to time, and continues an inspiration to me.

"Edward I." was bitter, is bitter. His memories are of excessive discipline, such as lying face down on the floor in front of a Jesuit priest, arms outstretched so his body made the shape of a cross, begging forgiveness for his misdeeds. His faith was broken and lost as he considered the priesthood, and he left Harlaxton.

"Keith S." has a more robust story. He was a bit older than the other novices, he decided that he didn't want to be cooped up as if in a prison, that he didn't want a life where girls were forbidden, and one day he just "put on my jacket and walked up the lane and out the front gates and never looked back." Ironically, he and his wife now live in Harlaxton village and are part of the Harlaxton church. He is a thoroughly fine man.

Intense stories, these. And these persons, too, are Harlaxton alums.

There are others.

The architect from St. Albans who stopped by the Manor on his way to a professional appointment in Edinburgh. As a child, he had lived at Harlaxton with his mother and father as part of a group of Polish immigrants who were working for the Jesuits, taking care of the property. He just wanted to see the place again.

Or the two women and one man, in nearby villages, who as children lived in the Gatehouse with their families while their fathers worked the estate. They remember Harlaxton in World War II, with the bombers landing at "RAF Harlaxton" behind the Manor.

Or Gerald Phyzackerly, who as a nine-year-old boy in 1939, just before Britain entered World War II, visited his great aunt Violet van der Elst at Harlaxton Manor, which she owned and called "Grantham Castle." Years later, as a distinguished clergyman in the Church of England, Rev. Phyzackerly told me of, then wrote of, his adventures exploring among the suits of armor and secret passages and rooms and woodlands of Harlaxton. What a playground for a boy! He, too, was an "alumnus" of Harlaxton and loved to return.

What was always puzzling to me was the absence of visits by persons who had been stationed at Harlaxton during World War II. The First British Airborne was one of the units at the Manor, and I always hoped one of these now-old gentlemen would stop by and, with a gleam in his eye, remember preparing for D-Day and the later air assault on Arnhem, the storied "bridge too far." Maybe he would show me the room he lived in, maybe we would stand together by the Pegasus Monument in its courtyard, maybe he would want to see the patriotic and homesick "graffiti" young airmen drew on walls of the tower above the Refectory, which we preserved when we renovated that space. But none of these "alumni" ever came, though members of the Parachute Regiment who had *not* lived at Harlaxton would visit. I always felt we were the lesser for not meeting any of the Harlaxton-based veterans.

For, you see, these persons were at or near the age of our present students. And they went out from the same rooms our students use now at Harlaxton to fight for our freedoms, to protect our liberties, to see their comrades die, to give hope to our world. It was, it is, no small thing.

I think about it sometimes, the "alumni" Harlaxton has nurtured. Airborne soldiers, soldiers of the cross, student dreamers and laborers in creating new worlds, summer students learning from their books and learning from travel in Britain and Europe. Harlaxton "alums" of all kinds, across all generations, all having done their parts in their own ways.

It is no wonder that the place inspires.

For Harlaxton is a crossroads of life, a crossroads of dreams.

This sketch also began as a report to the University of Evansville community through their weekly newsletter called AceNotes, this one for February 18, 2009. It is considerably adapted here.

Mohammed Led Me by the Hand Down Mt. Sinai

This is personal. More deeply personal than I can tell you here.

On the first long weekend of second semester, in February 2009, while students and faculty were traveling to Ireland on the College trip (and others, on their own, were going to Heidelberg and Paris and London and Oxford and Salisbury and Nottingham and Rome and Athens and Belgium and Norway and Cologne and Galway and Bath—all these places listed from our actual weekly check-out sheets), Suzanne and I slipped away to Egypt to climb Mt. Sinai.

I had long wished to climb both Mt. Olympus and Mt. Sinai, for it seems to me that all our spiritual and intellectual energy in the Western world suspends itself from these two peaks. Olympus symbolizes the Classical Traditions; Sinai stands for the Judeo-Christian Traditions. And that's who we are, in our heads and hearts.

A few years before, on an extended journey through Greece, we had managed to get a long way up Mt. Olympus before we ran into washed-out roads and trails. At least we were able to consort with some of the lesser Olympian gods, for a spell, in groves of ancient trees, rushing streams, and waterfalls whose echoes seemed to sound the destinies of all human life.

And this time, we reached the height, the tip-top, of Mt. Sinai—you know, burning bushes, tablets of the law, golden calf at the bottom, lusting for the fleshpots of Egypt, all of that. And we gazed in wonder at the barrenness of the Sinai Desert, all sand and stones, and listened to echoes of an ancient stillness.

It was a long climb, and hard. The trail was steep and treacherous, the land a scape of barren sand and rocks. Moses took those dudes to the middle of the desert, you know, a long, long way from anywhere — no wonder they rebelled!

Then, as we descended, it began to grow dark. We had only one tiny flashlight to share among us. Our Bedouin guide, required by the Egyptian government (I thought as a kind of make-work project for the Bedouin tribes in that part of the desert) had a tiny light on his cell phone. And that was it. Poor light, dangerous trail, a precarious situation. It was hard to see the rocky path, or to distinguish it from the false scree, the rubble and rock, that could lead you into danger. A broken leg or arm might be the best you could hope for if you lost your way. The adventure by foot that had been hard and long had now become dangerous as well. And therefore a bit frightening.

And then, in the darkness, unexpectedly, I felt the large hand of the Bedouin guide, a little guy named Mohammed, reaching out to me. I didn't expect it; it was a surprise, if not a shock. But I took it. I took his hand, placed my hand in the hand of Mohammed, trusted him, relied on him. And he led us safely the rest of the way down Sinai in the darkness, the stars above us so glittering bright and glorious that for the first time ever in our lives we understood, really, what the Psalmist was writing about.

I am still pondering this: "A Bedouin named Mohammed led me by the hand down Mt. Sinai."

For purposes of these sketches, I can and do turn this experience into a parable of what Harlaxton College is all about: new experience, openness to other people, acceptance of differing ways and faiths, understandings of a wholeness in the human family in this wide wide world, and — above all — a sense of our shared journey, our shared humanity.

Others from Harlaxton were grasping at this, in their own ways, in Heidelberg and Paris and London and Oxford and Salisbury and Nottingham and Rome and Athens and Belgium and Norway and Cologne and Galway and Bath and inside Harlaxton Manor itself.

Something powerful was going on, at Sinai, and something powerful was going on in every place a Harlaxton student was daring to dream and to do.

The fact is, something powerful was going on every day at Harlaxton Manor, so that every week was (in a tag line I frequently used in these reports) *just another quiet week at Harlaxton College, where all the faculty are brilliant, all the students are above average, and the energy never stops.*

True enough. But this experience in the gathering darkness on the dangerous rocky slope of Mt. Sinai was much more personal and meaning-full to me than just preaching a parable on Harlaxton College. It was an extraordinary moment, an extraordinary experience, of extraordinary power.

For you see, it had become a personal pilgrimage to me, for me, to climb Mt. Sinai, slow rocky risky step by slow rocky risky step, and ultimately to achieve the summit. And then to stand at the top of Sinai, gazing out on the wasteland of that desert wilderness, hearing echoes of God's words to Moses at the base of this mount—"Draw not nigh hither, for the place whereon thou standest is holy ground," knowing that this was the very place where it all began to take form for the children of Israel: their Law in the Ten Commandments, received and perceived in tablets of these very stones; their oh-so-human constant rebellion; their courage; their journey, always the journey, always the quest for the Promised Land. It is a Bible story; it is a human story.

I had paid my modest price in both spiritual and physical travail to complete this pilgrim's journey that, I knew, marked not an end, but a beginning: To stand on the summit of Sinai! What I did not know, could not have known, was that the true pilgrimage was yet to come.

In my pride, I was sure the descent would be easy and so didn't give it a thought—a lot easier to go down than up, isn't it? In my pride, I didn't count on the gathering darkness, the dangers—though now I see the lesson that in any pilgrimage of life the darkness and difficulties always come.

In my pride, I stepped into those dangers, danger of losing the way, danger of physical harm.

And then in the darkness, that unexpected help: a warm hand took mine, not the hand of a Moses, not the hand of a Jesus, but the hand of a stranger, a Bedouin named Mohammed. And it was he who led us through a dangerous darkness on a dangerous trail, brought us safely "home."

The stuff I had gone for—the ascent, the summit, the powerful story, the vision, the reverberations through the centuries of a man and a people meeting Jehovah God were there, were gained, were important, yes. But the deepest effect came as a surprise--through a touch of deliverance and safety, a hand in the darkness, the hand of a Bedouin tribesman named Mohammed.

He led. We followed.

And at that moment, something broke open; some deep wellsprings poured their deep and refreshing waters in that desert place of my heart. Something took place that was whole, complete, deep-down good. And right.

And the stars glittered even brighter in the dark desert sky.

"80" And "81"

It is common knowledge that George H. W. Bush and George W. Bush call each other, familiarly (as father and son ought so to do), "41" and "43," the elder having been the 41st President of the United States of America and "Dubya" having been the 43rd. George W. has even written a book with the title, *41: A Personal Biography of My Father*.

Now that's something. Quite a few somethings.

And Jeb Bush is just being heard from. (If only Barbara would have run!)

I'm not talking politics here, but just noting the fact that this remarkable family uses numbers both as identifiers and as shorthand, which has set me to musing on the numbers "80" and "81" in my own long and fortunate life, a life in which Harlaxton has played such an important part. As often with numbers, as the Bush family shows, they are markers.

So, I sit here in my little study on Turtle Creek in Beloit, Wisconsin, USA, on this my 81st birthday—November 22, 2014, remembering a year ago at Harlaxton Manor. And "80" and "81" become markers for one of life's great passages, the passage into what we call "retirement,"

I should back up a bit in the interests of clarity: I "retired" from William Jewell College in 1993 after twenty-seven years as Professor, Dean, and President. I was sixty years old. I proceeded to "flunk" that retirement, accepted a Vice-Presidency of Health Midwest, a dominant (fifteen-hospital) health care system in the Kansas City area, and worked there until late 2002 when they sold to "for-profit" Columbia HCA. I now retired again, aged sixty-nine.

Flunked that one, too. For at this point President Steve Jennings of the University of Evansville asked if I would go to their Harlaxton College campus in England as Principal, a place I knew well from establishing and sustaining a partnership between Harlaxton and

William Jewell over three decades. "Could you," President Jennings asked realistically, "maybe give us two or three years." I was to begin at Harlaxton January 1, 2003.

Suzanne and I went, leaving all we knew; we worked the two or three years as asked; things were going well; we were loving it; the home University was happy; and the two or three years extended themselves to nearly twelve, which put me at Harlaxton—or, actually, on a Harlaxton College field trip to London—on my 80th birthday.

"80"

And what a birthday! Suzanne had arranged with our students, probably through British faculty members Caroline Magennis and Edward Bujak and Graham Baker, that as I arrived to lead my student tours of St. Paul's Cathedral, the wonderful Harlaxton students would sing—from the huge steps of that monumental London church—"Happy Birthday to You, Happy Birthday to You, Happy Birthday Dr. Kingsley, Happy Birthday to You." Now could anyone anywhere in the whole wide world top that for a birthday greeting?! I was speechless (which is not my wont)!

Warmed by this brilliant live greeting card, I led my tours with a special zest and joy. Then we had a lovely birthday dinner in a fine London restaurant that night—Suzanne, friend John Ridley, and I— and the next morning John and I flew to Athens, where (after many months of running on the roads around Harlaxton to get ready, 'cause, hey, I am now 80) I ran from the Mound of the Marathon Warriors to the ancient Olympic Stadium in Athens. Ran quite a bit more than the 26.2 miles of Phidippides' original marathon route, 'cause I got lost a couple of times.

Friend John had persuaded the man with the key to let us into the locked Olympic Stadium, I ran a final lap there, and then John stood me up on the #1 level of the Olympic winners' podium for a photo op. Some Italian students who happened to be standing outside the gate in their orange ponchos—for it had been raining all day, some- times storming, making the marathon run all the more difficult— cheered enthusiastically as only Italian students can do:

"Bene!"

"Benissimo!"

Is that a birthday or what! "80."

And then back to work at Harlaxton, leading a fine little college for another half-year, with plans and meetings and dreams and visions and revisions and reports and telephone calls and e-mails and busy, busy days.

"81"

Then in due course, it all ended, as all must. Our choice. We had told the University a year and a half before that we would be retiring on June 30, 2014. So, late on that Monday afternoon we bade farewell to our friends and staff, who had gathered in the Great Entry Hall; took a Street Cars Taxi out the Great Front Gates; owner/driver Tom Morton took us to Grantham Station; we boarded the 16:40 East Coast train to London; and it was over. Just like that. All over.

Suddenly, instantly, we were no longer a part of Harlaxton College.

What now? We traveled in the Baltics — Latvia, Lithuania, Estonia, and even Finland — for a couple of weeks, spent some days at our little Irish cottage in County Donegal, then the big step: beginning to settle into a home in the woods on Turtle Creek in Beloit, Wisconsin, USA, where we knew and were known by virtually no one.

It has taken awhile to get used to the freedom: no meetings, no reports, few external demands. Suzanne has been creating a beautiful house out of this interesting property in this favored location. I have been patient about "what is next," not rushing to "get involved" or "do things." I retrieved from my seldom-opened man's "jewelry" box some cufflinks Suzanne had once given me — does anyone wear cufflinks any more? I guess they do — and put them in a little ceremonial glass goblet on my desk, along with a £2 coin which has engraved on its rim Isaac Newton's much-too-humble explanation of his scientific greatness: "I was," he said, "Standing on the Shoulders of Giants."

The legend on the cufflinks is more appropriate to my current situation as "81." The left one says "Been There." The right one says "Done That." And for now, we'll leave it right there.

I don't feel old—but then that's what my Canadian grandmother, Cora Evalena Stone Payne, told me on her 100th birthday. I am still a bit mystified about how on "80" you can be immensely useful, leading a college, as busy-busy-busy as the native animals in our woods on Turtle Creek, and on "81" become in the collective minds of "what the martyrs call the world" a used and useless commodity, finished, done, toast, gone, marginalized, meaningless.

Thousands, millions have gone through this process before. Some get noisy and talk about who they were, what they did. Others insist on wearing equally loud, out-of-style clothes and getting into discussion groups with weird names where they damn the present generations. Still others, more productively, "volunteer"—but an academic person feels like he has been part volunteer all his life, and in any case I think it would be hard to find fulfillment in punching the tickets when I was accustomed to putting on the whole drama.

No, I think for the time being I'll just enjoy the seasons changing on Turtle Creek, and the deer and wild turkeys and squirrels and waterfowl, and write these little sketches about Harlaxton, and some more stuff that may be useful to the archives of both William Jewell and Harlaxton, including a memoir that might even someday be interesting to some family member.

There was an 81st birthday celebration today, not in London and Athens, of course, but here in Beloit, Wisconsin. This time, Suzanne's "choir" was two beautiful grandbabies, Harper-Almost-Three and Brooklyn-Almost-Five, who rushed in from a "secret" shopping expedition excitedly offering colorful birthday cards and a huge plastic jar of cashew nuts and a reading light for travel and two—not one, but *two*—boxes of "your favorite candy, Grandpa." Junior Mints. They even offered to help eat them. And the meal was not at a posh London restaurant but at Applebee's. And the birthday journey was not to Marathon and Athens, but--knees now not so good after fifty years of running and after last year's quaint marathonic excess—a little walk out back, in the Thanksgiving week snows, joining the other semi-tame creatures along Turtle Creek.

Not so exciting as "80." But not so bad, not so bad.

I am inspired by Monet, old by the standards of his day and nearly blind, still creating his gardens at Giverny from river wasteland, then creating them again in his art, including one after another of those magnificent *Water Lilies* in l'Orangerie and Marmottan Galleries in Paris.

And I am inspired by the Irish poet William Butler Yeats, who wrote in his old age, in his great poem "Sailing to Byzantium," the words,

> An aged man is but a paltry thing,
> A tattered coat upon a stick, unless
> Soul clap its hands and sing, . . .

No, "81" is not so bad at all on Turtle Creek. For I know in my deep soul how I worked, how hard and purposefully I worked, joining with others to create some very lovely gardens: they are called "Jewell" and "Harlaxton." And now I have the leisure to write about them, to transmute reality into the colors and shapes and rhythms and meanings of words, perhaps with insights that are new or at the least newly shared.

And all the while I am blessed beyond measure—thank you for giving it words, W.B. Yeats—that still, still, every morning, my soul claps its hands—and sings.

And so I sit here, warmed with what Yeats called "mighty memories," memories of Harlaxton on "80" and thousands, millions of warm memories from before that day. And the wise mute objects in the little ceremonial goblet on my desk find a voice to whisper "Don't forget."

For I, too, have had the privilege of standing on the shoulders of some giants in my own time, in my own line of work. And I, too, know the great joy of having

"Been There!"

"Done That!"

Poetry and Song

Of course, Harlaxton inspires poetry and song. Of course she does.

Some of it doggerel, either on purpose or "can't help it." Some of it quite good. And all of it passionately sincere or whimsically fun.

I've collected some of it over my years with Harlaxton — whatever I could, whenever I could. Much much more of it got away, as it does, for it is all so intensely personal.

Mike Carson, Arthur Brown, and Rob Griffith of the University of Evansville are among the academic poets I know who "sang Harlaxton," writing about everything from British Studies lectures to a tractor working the farm field beyond to the Monday pheasant shoots.

At a much lower level, we had a "Harlaxton Birthday Song" that we would roll out on occasion to the embarrassed pleasure of the student or staff member so "honored," singing it to the tune of "The Volga Boatman."

> Happy Birthday. Happy Birthday.
> Sin and sickness in the air,
> People dying everywhere,
> Happy Birthday. Happy Birthday.

Former Harlaxton faculty member Chris Whitehead, from his teaching post at the University of Newcastle, embellished this masterpiece with further dismal verses.

Alan Holiman of William Jewell wrote a ballad of "Margaret Thatcher, Milk Snatcher," to the tune of "Deck the Halls with Boughs of Holly" which premiered in a British Studies class on a day when the lecture was about that strong Prime Minister from Grantham (and when, unfortunately, an Academic Vice President was visiting from Evansville).

The ditty begins,

Margaret Thatcher walks on water
  Fa la la la la, la la la la,
From Grantham town a grocer's daughter
  Fa la la la la, la la la la . . . . and so on.

Cheryl Waclaw, J. Livingston, and Jeff Reed came up with a "Golden Gong Song" with a chorus that celebrated and/or satirized the gong that began British Studies lectures, along with some of the academic symbols and slogans of the time:

Big red "L", golden gong,
It's time to learn all together.
Hit the gong, wow the throng,
Enjoy your time at Harlaxton.

Prof. Will Denson in 1997 celebrated the naked mile, as a professor might, by deciding in verse *not* to run it (though his professor-colleague Mike Carson apparently did). After five very clever stanzas he concludes,

I'd have done the naked mile,
I'd have bravely done the task;
I'd have loped beside Doc Carson —
But, thank God, he didn't ask.

Because then I got to thinking
"Man, this night air sure is cold;"
Life's a long way to the highway,
I'm afraid I'm way too old.

In addition to the "fun" verses, there are love songs to Harlaxton, including Raymond Zupp's "My Love, My Home, My Harlaxton" and Sally Brown's "Blessed Harlaxton, My Home"; there are poems of inspiration as in Dana Monroe Samson's "Towering Moments at Harlaxton Manor" or Gary J. Beolhower's 1999 lyric on "Lost in Harlaxton Manor," which concludes with an experience many have embraced:

Rooms upon rooms –
my soul gives up its secrets

and provides passages to new knowing.

In this grand manor
I am lost forever
and forever found.

Prof. Kay Gandy of Western Kentucky University captures the "Harlaxton changed my life" refrain that many of us have experienced in her "Farewell Song" from 2012:

My time has ended at Harlaxton
I came because I heard it was fun
I didn't know when the time was done
My life would change
Be rearranged
Never the same
Since Harlaxton

O Harlaxton, O Harlaxton
Didn't know what I could be . . . .

I conclude this sampler with a very fine work by a very fine poet from the University of Southern Indiana, Matthew Graham, who along with his equally fine artist wife Katie Waters has given *to* and taken *from* Harlaxton in just the way it is supposed to happen. This is Matthew's "The Conservatory" from 2008, important to me not only because of the sheer artistry that speaks through the images Matthew molds, shapes, connects, but also for the very pedestrian and very sacred reason that the Conservatory was the first part of the Manor that we helped bring back from ruin, beginning in 2003, with Suzanne's courage-in-adversity leading the way.

THE CONSERVATORY

Rain, then dappled light against the leaded glass.
The day lingers here, conserved among the palms.
The stone path, and shaded statuary.
Let the day linger
Like an unfinished letter left on a writing desk
Beside a vase of jonquils

In an upstairs sitting room.
From the Great Hall the first notes of a piano
Rise and then fall,
Then rise and fall again
Like the breath of someone sleeping.
The air in here is old.
The air in here is old yet as stubborn
As the crippled swan
Guarding the ornamental pond
Beyond the dripping yews,
As insistent as the cuttings
Taken from Kew Gardens
That whisper
Persist, no matter.
And then wind
And more English rain against the trembling glass.

"Blessed Harlaxton, My Home" and Sally B.

She is magical, a pied piper, a teacher-musician who engages and inspires and brings both the music and her students to a new life, a new vitality.

Sally Brown is her name, and for a period of years we were blessed to have her as our faculty colleague and Director of the Harlaxton Collegiate Choir.

Before Sally B. came, our choir would be led by a faculty or spouse volunteer—an engineer, a violinist, someone who had sung in a church choir sometime. You get the picture. They did good work, kept music alive, made opportunities for Harlaxton students.

Then one day Sally B. stopped by Harlaxton Manor. Sally led some community choirs in the area, one with the arresting name the "Out of Silence Choir" (because they sang music of the "silent" women and servants in great houses like Harlaxton, which Sally had researched and brought to light--therefore "out of silence") and another named the "Choir Invisible" (I don't know the story of that one—could it be, I wonder, from the George Eliot poem, "O May I Join the Choir Invisible?"). These community choirs were award winning; one of them placed high in the annual BBC choirs competition; one sang before Nelson Mandela, who became a patron—you get the picture.

Sally had in earlier years trained as a sculptress and was successful in that art, then "traveled with a jazz outfit" for a while playing string bass and other instruments. She is a remarkably versatile person, an artist and writer as well as musician. She needed a place for her choirs to rehearse. We needed a choirmaster. And so we set up a barter arrangement, overriding the protectiveness of our staff toward their/our manor house, assuming some of the inconveniences of having an "outside group" using Harlaxton, and brought music, blessed music, into a house that was made for music. They were beautiful days and nights at Harlaxton Manor!

And that's how Sally Brown became Director of the Harlaxton Collegiate Choir. She was good. So inspiring was she that up to half our students each semester, always at least a third, signed up to sing. Sally worked well with our British Studies faculty and our Student Development staff, linking the choir to the whole range of Harlaxton life. It was brilliant. Simply brilliant. And for several good years.

Then, alas, Sally B. had some health problems, she and her doctors knew she was overextended, and she wisely cut back her schedule. Her choirs moved to another practice venue, and she passed the Harlaxton Collegiate Choir on to other excellent musicians, first to Dr. Phil Taylor of our British Studies Faculty and then to Cambridge-trained Dr. Tim Williams.

But before leaving, she wrote for her Harlaxton choir these words in October, 2007, blending two folk tunes to create the music. Her song, to me, says all that needs to be said:

THE HARLAXTON SONG

When the dark'ning clouds of sorrow
Gather threat'ning in the sky,
Lend the light that I might follow,
Bring your spirit to my side.
  No storm can shake my inmost calm
  While to that rock I'm clinging;
  It sounds an echo in my soul:
  How can I keep from *calling*
For your quiet grace, for your golden face
Blessèd Harlaxton, my home;
On the foaming sea, speaking peace to me,
How your loving arms enfold.

There the voices raised in sweetness
Where the painted angels throng,
Should I falter in my purpose
I recall that gladsome song.
  No storm can shake my inmost calm
  While to that rock I'm clinging;

It sounds an echo in my soul:
How can I keep from *singing*
In those quiet halls, as the ev'ning falls,
Blessèd Harlaxton, my home,
Heav'n's bright stars conspire, with that distant choir
To dispel the dark unknown.

There the youthful dreams find courage
In the tow'rs of ancient stone,
There the flow'rs of wisdom flourish,
Kindly knowledge, gently grown.
   No storm can shake my inmost calm
   While to that rock I'm clinging;
   It sounds an echo in my soul:
   How can I keep from *dreaming*
Of your quietness, England's fruitfulness,
Blessèd Harlaxton, my home;
Take my thankful heart
As your child departs
Whence the westward winds are blown.

About the Author

Dr. J. Gordon Kingsley is one of few persons privileged to lead colleges in both America and Britain, having served as the twelfth President of William Jewell College in Missouri and the sixth Principal of Harlaxton College in England. In between college gigs, he served as a Vice President for Health Midwest and Deputy Director of the Nelson-Atkins Museum of Art, both in Kansas City.

While he was leading William Jewell, an Exxon-funded study adjudged him to be among the top 5% of America's "most effective collegiate leaders." He subsequently received an appointment as Visiting Fellow at Cambridge University.

He holds four doctorates, earned and honorary, from universities in America and Japan; has served numerous civic, educational, and religious boards in America and Britain; has been an active public speaker "whose presentations combine stirring advocacy of fundamental values for our time with frequent touches of rather wretched humor"; and has written four previous books: *A Time for Openness (1971); Frontiers: The Story of Missouri Baptists (1983); Conversations with Leaders for a New Millennium (1991); and A Place Called Grace (1992).*

And all that, plus £4.05, might get him a Medium Americano with hot milk and a blueberry muffin at Costa's Coffee Shop in Grantham.

He and his wife Suzanne, a former Collegiate Vice President of William Jewell College, now live in retirement on Turtle Creek in Beloit, Wisconsin.

45494476R00109

Made in the USA
San Bernardino, CA
09 February 2017